# ALL I
# CAN DO
# IS PRAY

D1255457

# ALL I CAN DO IS PRAY

## Discovering the Power of Prayer

JULIE CICORA

WESTBOW®
PRESS
A DIVISION OF THOMAS NELSON
& ZONDERVAN

WestBow Press books may be ordered through booksellers or by contacting:

WestBow Press
A Division of Thomas Nelson & Zondervan
1663 Liberty Drive
Bloomington, IN 47403
www.westbowpress.com
1 (866) 928-1240

ISBN: 978-1-4908-7712-9 (sc)
ISBN: 978-1-4908-7714-3 (hc)
ISBN: 978-1-4908-7713-6 (e)

Library of Congress Control Number: 2015906002

Print information available on the last page.

WestBow Press rev. date: 04/21/2015

*To my loving husband, Scott*

# Foreword

These stories are true. However all the names and sometimes the gender of the patients have been changed to protect their privacy. I am most grateful to these patients who welcomed me into some of the most private and profound moments of their lives and deaths.

# Chapter One

I didn't believe in prayer at the beginning of that summer; I believed in action. I had no idea what to expect when I entered the small conference room at the hospital for the first time, and that made me nervous. A white plastic table spattered with coffee stains and surrounded by mismatched chairs took up the majority of the room. Three of the windowless walls were covered with bookshelves, and on the fourth wall was a dingy white board with the words *Clinical Pastoral Education* at the top. This was a long way from the spacious, highly polished mahogany boardrooms I was used to from my corporate life. A few people had already taken a place at the table. I squeezed past an athletic-looking younger man with a mop of bushy black hair, knocking some books off a shelf in the process. As I stooped to pick them up, I looked around at the new group of student chaplains accepted into the hospital's three-month Clinical Pastoral Education program. There were both men and women ranging in age from their late twenties to early sixties. Some looked bored, others expectant, but none looked as apprehensive as I felt. This program was mandatory for the ordination process in the Episcopal Church. And since I felt compelled to become an Episcopal priest, here I was. This calling had become apparent six years earlier and had somehow lodged itself in my head like a tiny sliver causing me constant irritation. It was only when I paid attention to the desire to become a priest that I felt relief. I had no idea where the idea had come from, only that I needed to do something about it. A discernment committee from my church had been appointed to journey with me as I explored my sense of call. In the beginning it made no sense at all to me. I was happily pursuing a successful career in sales, I was in a second marriage to a wonderful man, and I was raising five sons between my husband's children and my own. The committee ended up affirming my call to the ministry, and to my surprise, so did my husband. I began taking classes part-time in the local seminary, and soon I was hooked. The Bible was one of the most stimulating subjects I had ever studied. After six years, I had completed most of the laundry list of requirements for the priesthood.

I just had one problem, and in a few minutes, I was going to have to confess it. The program director had finished his introductory remarks and had given us instructions on how to introduce ourselves and talk about what we wanted to study during the session. My colleagues were talking about deepening their spirituality, learning how to be pastoral, studying the various stages of grief, and other appropriate topics that would help them become more competent ministers.

Then it was my turn, my time to confess a very unpriestly kind of problem. In a calm and—I hoped—confident voice, I said, "I don't believe in the power of prayer." The faces at the table looked blank. It was as if they hadn't heard me correctly. They probably thought I'd said the exact opposite. I continued: "Not believing in prayer is a problem for me since I'm called to do it all the time, so I thought I would study prayer."

"Huh. Oh, okay." My supervisor, Ted, a member of the Russian Orthodox Church, made a note and then peered over his reading glasses at the next person. Ted had a round face full of freckles, and his reddish-blond hair was heavily mixed with gray and surrounded his head like a monk's tonsure. It was like looking at Yoda, and I found his non-judgmental presence calming. His pen moved across the page slowly and methodically as he wrote down what each chaplain wanted to put in his or her learning contract, one of the many requirements needed to get credit in the Clinical Pastoral Education program, or CPE for short.

"Whoa, just a minute." Nick, the young, athletic man I had climbed over to find a seat, was holding up both hands like a cop stopping traffic. He had introduced himself as a staunch Baptist. "How can you be in the ordination process and not believe in prayer?" He was breathing hard, and the words came out in little bursts of air. As I would soon learn, for Nick, prayer was as necessary as oxygen, water, and food. He thrived on it. He was the Mozart of prayer. Most of our meetings started with a prayer, and when Nick prayed, he would hunker down in his chair, close his eyes tightly, open his hands, and beginning in a soft, deep, melodious voice, he would call upon Jesus. As he prayed, his voice would crescendo from a barely audible pianissimo to a window-rattling forte punctuated by exclamations of "our Lord," finally reaching a triple forte "amen" resembling one of the cannon shots at the end of the 1812 overture. I actually liked how he prayed. It was hard not to be caught up in his passion. He always prayed for the individual needs of the group, and he always prayed for me, that my heart would be open to the work of God through prayer. What I didn't like was his need to turn us all into another version of him.

Because of Nick's passion for prayer, the group ran into a major interfaith snag. Because we started each meeting with prayer, this caused a problem with one of the chaplains who was Unitarian and didn't believe in a "God." She also did not want to have the Christians in the group invoke the name of Jesus. This was like telling Nick that he would not be able to use his arms and legs. As we hammered out the rules for praying, our supervisor sat back and watched. This was part of the CPE process: handling conflict. And there clearly was conflict.

Beth, our resident Unitarian, was very clear about her beliefs. "I know there is energy in the universe that can be used for good, but I'm offended when you insist on calling it Jesus." She sat upright in her chair, her fingers clasped in front of her, her thin body rigid like she was poised to take a punch. She was a tall woman, midforties, with closely cropped red hair that seemed like an accessory to her purple-beaded earrings. She wore a sapphire-blue dress that reminded me of a bathing suit cover-up. Hot pink running shoes completed her outfit.

Nick shook his head back and forth, his shaggy black hair hiding his round, dark, Disney eyes, and looked at the rest of the Christians around the table for support. "Well, I'm offended when you call God en–er–gy!" He spat out each syllable.

The arguing continued. I kept waiting for our supervisor, Ted, to weigh in. After all, I assumed as an Orthodox Christian, he was all about the power of Jesus. Why didn't he stop this crazy dialogue and tell us what to do instead of just calmly sitting there. With the mounting tension, sweat was beginning to form all over my body. The arguing was causing my shoulders to creep up toward my ears, and I could feel my back beginning to tighten. Episcopalians, my denomination, are taught to be polite in a religious setting. We don't raise our voices and are uncomfortable with confrontation. In the boardroom, I would have welcomed the chance to spar with my customer. But in this environment, my response was to lower my head so there would be no eye contact. As the only person to confess she didn't believe in prayer, I felt that I had no business offering an opinion on how to pray.

"This disagreement about the opening prayer is really not a problem," offered Judy, a sixty-year-old nun who had just returned from missionary work in Malaysia. I still hadn't figured out why she was taking Clinical Pastoral Education. "Why don't we each pray in our own traditional way? We can take turns opening our meetings. This will give us the opportunity to experience different ways of praying." She had a teacher's voice: the tone conveyed an expectation of obedience. She wore a starched white cotton shirt and a plain blue skirt like a habit. She held her head as if she still wore the veil from long ago.

The group silently considered that option.

"But I'm the only Unitarian. The rest of you are Christian. I'm going to be buried in Christianity," Beth whined.

"Suck it up, Beth," Judy said. And so ended the argument.

As for my statement about not believing in the power of prayer, Nick was appalled, Beth felt like she might have gained an ally, Judy was bored, and Frank, a sixty-five-year-old Roman Catholic priest, seemed uninterested—he sat back reading the program requirements. I tried to explain my position on prayer.

"All I'm saying, Nick, is that I don't really understand prayer and how it works, if it works at all. I'm used to being able to do something about problems. Prayer, at this moment, seems like a cop-out. If someone is sick or dying, there's really nothing I can do about it as a chaplain except pray, and what does that do?"

Nick took a deep breath. "Well, for starters—"

"Let's go to our assigned units," Ted interrupted.

Good, Ted had rescued me from a lecture by Nick. I picked up my notebook and my little zippered black Bible and climbed the seven floors to my assigned unit: oncology. Using the stairs was going to be one of the few ways I was going to get exercise this summer. Nick followed me but chose instead to take the elevator. He was assigned to the intensive care unit (ICU) on the eighth floor.

Ted had given each chaplain a list of patients. The list showed their names, ages, and diagnoses. The first name on my list was Robert Allen, fifty-eight years old, diagnosis: liver cancer, terminal. I found his room. Robert Allen was listed in bed B, the farthest from the door. Bony feet that looked like they had been dipped in wax were all that were visible at the end of the dividing curtain. All they needed was a toe tag. I inched my way around the curtain to the end of the bed, wondering what exactly I would find. A dead body?

"Hi, Mr. Allen, how are you?" I addressed the still form under the covers, trying to sound nice without being overly cheerful. I clutched my little black Bible and made sure my hospital ID was visible.

"Who are you?" he asked very softly. He lay on his side facing away from the door. The skin on his arm looked like paper that was at least one hundred years old. A knitted cap covered his head, and a thin, dingy white hospital sheet covered the rest of his body. The room was bare—no cards, no flowers, and nothing on his table with the exception of one picture. It was a picture of a house on a lake.

"I'm Julie, the chaplain." I sat down in the chair facing him.

"Well, I don't believe in God." He'd pulled the blanket at the end of his bed over his feet. "I'm cold."

Oh, thank God, I thought and started toward the door.

"You don't have to leave. You can still talk to me." His voice was strained, and he sounded almost breathless.

"Okay," I said.

I stared at the Bible on my lap. I had no idea what to do next. This was my first interaction with a patient, and already I was at a loss. I felt totally incompetent. In my "other life" I had been in corporate sales—twenty years of account calls, presentations in boardrooms, and solving customer problems. Now, I was making small talk with a terminal patient. I had taken a leave of absence from my job to complete this unit of Clinical Pastoral Education. The process for holy orders in my diocese required it. Three months of giving pastoral care, working through conflicts brought about by my fellow chaplains, and dealing with all my own stuff that would surface because I lived in a crisis-filled environment. I felt helpless as I looked at the man in the bed. He was dying of cancer, he didn't believe in God, and he was cold.

"Can I get you another blanket?" The problem solver in me had kicked in.

"Won't help. It doesn't matter how many blankets I put on this bed; I just can't seem to get warm." His clawlike fingers pulled his knitted cap farther down over his ears. His bones practically poked through his paperlike skin.

"Oh."

That was it. All I could say was oh? I didn't know what to do. I didn't know where to look, and I certainly didn't know what to say.

I could see my own discomfort reflected in his eyes. He took pity on me. "Since you're the chaplain, why don't you just say a little prayer?"

"Okay." I leaned forward. Should I take his hand?

Again, I was at a total loss. What should I pray for? The man was terminal. It said so on my patient sheet. I resorted to my sales background. Always find out what the customer wants first.

"What would you like me to pray for?" I asked.

He squinted and glanced at the picture of the house. "Well, I would like to go home to die, but for some reason, the doctor won't let me. Why don't you ask your God to let me go home?"

I took his hand, closed my eyes, and said, "Please, God, let Mr. Allen go home. Amen."

At that moment, the dividing curtain fluttered, and a large man appeared at the end of the bed. His white lab coat was peppered with coffee stains, and he was holding three thick patient charts that had forms and papers sticking out in all directions. Underneath the embroidered logo of the hospital was the word oncology in thick black letters. "Bob, I was just walking down the hallway, considering the idea of sending you home, and I felt compelled to come in here and tell you that I've changed my mind. I'll contact hospice, and we'll make the arrangements to get you out of here."

Mr. Robert Allen looked at me and smiled. "Wow, you're good."

# Chapter Two

"Ted!"

I threw open the door to his office, causing a stack of journals to collapse. I had wasted no time running down the seven flights of stairs and winding my way through the maze of hallways to my supervisor's office. His office was small and narrow. Like the conference room, there was just enough room for a desk and two chairs. At least this room had a window that overlooked a small courtyard. Ted was sitting in a chair next to the window eating a salad. I sat in the empty chair directly in front of him. Our knees almost touched. "You're never going to believe what just happened to me."

He stopped chewing, a look of amusement on his face. "Okay, I'll bite; what just happened?"

"You're never going to believe this …" I told him the story about Mr. Allen.

Ted sat there calmly picking the black olives out of his salad and piling them on the desk, listening and nodding. When I finished, he said, "That's wonderful, Julie, but you should probably get back up to your unit."

I stared at him and thought, that's it?

He picked up a journal. Did nothing faze this guy? I wanted an explanation. Why had the doctor walked in at that very moment and offered to let Mr. Allen go home? Ted sat there with a "been

8

there done that attitude" as if I had just told him the most boring story in the world.

I was waiting for some additional reaction, but then I remembered how he had been at our first meeting. An interview was part of the program application process for CPE. When I found his office, Ted was flipping through the pages of my spiritual autobiography. I watched him read for a few minutes before clearing my throat to let him know I was there. I needed to get into this program in order to be ordained as an Episcopal priest. This was the last step in a very long list of requirements.

"So," he had started. "I see that you moved around a lot as a child. What was that like for you?"

The question had startled me. I had never really considered how I felt about moving so much. I had just accepted it.

"Well, for one thing, I don't have any life-long friends," suddenly feeling, for the first time, the loss that comes with moving: the times of saying good-bye to friends, packing up, and leaving familiar places. I remembered staring at the empty rooms, feeling a similar emptiness inside. Tears were beginning to form, and I felt one slowly make its way down my cheek. My hands were clenched in my lap.

Ted was silent, watching me. "I'm sure it was very difficult for you."

The tears were falling faster by that time, and my lower lip quivered. I couldn't believe I was crying. I never cry and certainly not in front of other people. I sat there struggling to regain my composure.

"What are you feeling right now?" Ted had asked.

"Sadness," I said.

"I would imagine so, but we can spend more time talking about this after you start as a chaplain."

It took a few moments for me to process that he had just told me I had been accepted into the program. Just like now, I remembered waiting patiently for him to elaborate. After a few moments of silence, I realized the interview was over. I got up and left.

Back in the present moment, I was staring at Ted's half-eaten salad sitting on top of a stack of manila folders next to his chair. Still seemingly absorbed in his journal, I wondered if he even knew I was still there.

"Ted, doesn't that surprise you at all? I mean I make a statement that I'm going to study the power of prayer and less than thirty minutes later there is this incredible coincidence?"

"No, I'm not really surprised. You seem to have a lot of these coincidences going on in your life." He kept reading.

"What do you mean?"

He put down the journal. "Well, let's take the story you told me about how you got permission to take time off from your corporate job to do the chaplaincy." He got up, stretched, and said, "I have a meeting."

Chagrined, I sat in the quiet of his office, thinking back to the previous September. I had gone to my sales manager to ask for three months leave in order to enroll in the Clinical Pastoral Education Program. My manager had been sitting in his office, hidden behind a large computer screen. His desk was covered with papers, spreadsheets, brochures, and magazines. A coffee cup was balanced on top of a bunch of binders that I recognized as our sales team's fourth-quarter marketing plans, a reality check that made me think I had probably been naive to think that I would get all this time off without a hassle. I had been feeling entitled since I planned to use my twelve weeks of vacation. Unfortunately, my manager was not at all supportive.

"You want to do what? Take off May, June, and July next year? How nice it would be if we all could have the summer off. Now, tell me again; why do you want three months off?"

"I need to complete a unit of clinical pastoral education. It's part of my ordination process."

"Well," he said impatiently. He stood and his suit coat fell off the back of his chair. His shirt was wrinkled, and he reached up and loosened his tie. "How do you think I'm going to make my quota if one of my reps is off working somewhere else? Have you given any thought to who would cover your accounts?" His round face began to turn red, and sweat stains were clearly visible under his arms as he paced back and forth. He was livid.

But I knew this question was coming, so I was prepared. Waving a thick document at him, I said, "I have a coverage plan right here that should work."

"No. Absolutely not." He pointed to the marketing plans and leaned toward me, his face level with mine. "A territory like yours cannot be managed with a coverage plan." He was almost growling.

Now I was angry. "Can we discuss this further to see if we can reach an agreement that will satisfy both our needs?"

The phone rang. Glaring at me, he picked up the receiver and began talking. I sat there until he motioned me out.

How dare he, I fumed as I walked back to my desk and sat down. It was September. Somehow, I needed to keep my job and take off three months next year. How was I going to do this? I needed my income. My husband, Scott, and I were both on a second marriage. Between us, we had five sons. My husband's boys were in Maryland, where he shared custody with his former wife, and my boys were in New York, where I had joint custody with their father. Scott maintained an apartment in Maryland and went every other weekend to spend time with his boys. A house in New York, an apartment in Maryland, and five kids were not cheap. I couldn't afford to quit. God was going to have to make this happen.

In the past couple of years at seminary I had tried to begin a dialogue with God, but I felt like I was talking to myself. The experience seemed totally one-sided. I knew I was supposed to be in relationship with God, but I wasn't quite sure how to do it. I felt some kind of presence there, but I couldn't access it. Prayer was a way of thinking out loud inside my head. The only time I felt called to pray was when I needed something. But now, I was angry. "Okay, God. If you want me to get ordained, I need your help in making this happen." Looking back, I'm not quite sure how I expected God to help, but a few moments later, the phone rang at my desk.

"Julie Cicora speaking," I said.

"Julie, it's Kurt. I'm calling because there's a new job opening up in New York at one of the distributors. They're looking for a rep in your location, and I thought you would be great."

I had known Kurt a long time. He had previously been in sales but was now managing a distribution account.

"What made you think of me?" I couldn't believe he had called me just as I was wondering what to do.

"I don't know," he said. "I had this hunch you might need a change."

He had caught me at the right moment. I wasn't thinking clearly at first about just what a massive change this would be. I had been taking care of my current accounts for over ten years and had built strong relationships with my customers based on trust and loyalty. There were few surprises in my territory. At the beginning of the month, I knew exactly which accounts would give me the business needed to make my quota. Taking on a new job would mean starting over and building a new customer base, a process that would require a lot more time and effort on my part. How could the uncertainty of a new job possibly be a better path? Besides, why would I expect a new manager to be more willing to give me three months off than my current supervisor? The whole situation seemed crazy, but I was in a crazy frame of mind, so I applied for the job.

Two weeks later, I was on the early morning flight to New York City with four other reps from the office, who were also applying for the job. They were all good sales people, but we seemed to be avoiding each other; we all sat in different parts of the plane. When we shared a cab, I tried to make conversation, but no one wanted to talk. I began to realize that this was a coveted job opportunity.

As luck would have it, my interview was last. I hung out at the company's office on the fifty-fifth floor of a tall Manhattan skyscraper and pretended to work. This whole idea was ridiculous.

I had never planned on going into the ministry until I stumbled into a class at the divinity school. I had been on a sales call at a large corporation that turned out to be a total waste of time. After I was done, I found myself wandering through an unfamiliar neighborhood graced with a beautiful set of buildings. It was January in Upstate New York, which means gray, damp, and depressing. January is also my birthday month, and I had been feeling stagnant. The buildings were the only beautiful sight in what was otherwise a cloudy day, so I decided to find out what they were. I went inside, and the receptionist told me it was a school. Not quite sure why, I found myself signing up for a class. When I went to the class, I discovered everyone was studying for the ministry. I had no idea what I was doing there, but it had led me to this current irrationality, interviewing for a totally new job just so I could get three months off to complete a crucial part of my ordination process. I wanted to be satisfied with my corporate job, but this feeling was secondary to the inner desire for something more that was propelling me toward the ministry. A new energy present in my life since I had discerned my calling was putting my senses into overdrive. To my eyes, the sky was an impossible electric blue, and the trees were in high definition, each leaf in detail almost like a fingerprint. To my nose, the musty scent of the earth and the heady aroma of fresh-cut grass were as enticing as the smell of freshly baked bread. To my skin, humidity felt like a soothing wind-blown caress. I perceived the world in a way I had never experienced before. This energy-heightened sense of awareness stayed with me, propelling me through all my classes at seminary, and now it was solidifying. I was determined to make this chaplaincy work.

I watched as four men in their suits and newly shined shoes went in and out of the conference room. They were there for about an hour each, and when they came out, they looked straight ahead, avoiding my eyes. I began to despair when the last candidate emerged with a large folder and a pile of papers with the account's annual report on the top.

I got up from my chair and paced back and forth. My hands got clammy. I hadn't really done any research on the job or the account. All of a sudden, I had a feeling that I really needed this job because it might be the only way I could manage to do the chaplaincy, and I was unprepared.

The conference room door opened, and out stepped the hiring manager. She was from California, near the account headquarters. Her blonde hair fit my California stereotype, but the rest was all Manhattan. Black suit, black heels, black Coach bag, and the corporate white silk blouse.

"Julie?" She looked at me. "Mary Pat," she said sticking out her hand. As we walked into the conference room, she put her arm around my shoulder and whispered, "Let's get out of here." She stuffed her cell phone and laptop into her briefcase and grabbed her coat. The materials from the last candidate were lying on the table. She swept them into the garbage can and turned to me with a smile. "Ready?"

When we hit the ground floor, she said, "I know a great place. The Monkey Room." She took off. I almost had to run to keep up with her.

The Monkey Room turned out to be a trendy, upscale restaurant just around the corner from the office. Mary Pat swept into the restaurant with the energy of the Santa Anna winds. The restaurant walls were covered with murals depicting jungle scenes. The place was jammed with people. The hostess guided us to a small table. "I'll have a Cosmo," Mary Pat announced.

I thought, You go, girl. This job opportunity was starting to feel right. When the twenty-something waitress asked what I wanted to drink, I said, "A Cosmo sounds good to me," not having a clue what it was. I didn't have anything to lose. I waited patiently while Mary Pat reapplied her lipstick.

"Well, do you want the job?" She looked at me over the lipstick mirror. I found out later she had called every one of my accounts and talked to my customers. She knew about my customer relationships, how much I had grown the sales in my territory, and how I had done it. She wanted me on her team.

"Yes, but I need three months off next May, June, and July," I squeezed my eyes shut.

"Sure. Not a problem," Mary Pat said. It was almost like she hadn't heard me. Our drinks had arrived, and Mary Pat proceeded to order pasta for each of us. After firing off the lunch order, she launched into a long speech about what needed to be done with the account. Her speech was staccato with a trace of a Long Island accent. She would stop occasionally to comment on someone's shoes or hairstyle. She looked at anything that caught her attention, and everything did.

In between bites of pasta, she explained that the account was headquartered in Los Angeles, and I was being hired to cover the site in Buffalo. My job was to spend my time helping the telemarketing sales force sell more of our hardware. The sales team on the West Coast would handle new product introductions, contract negotiations, and marketing. The second her pasta was done, Mary Pat motioned to the waitress, and within minutes, a towering mound of quivering chocolate mousse appeared. Seconds later, another waitress placed a piece of New York style cheesecake in front of me. It was huge and dripping with strawberry sauce. Looking directly at me after sampling the mousse she asked, "Now, why do you need three months off?"

So she had heard me. "I'm studying to be an Episcopal priest, and I need to complete a three-month program in clinical pastoral education."

Her eyes narrowed. "And then what; you quit your sales job and save the world?"

"Oh no, I still have five kids to get through college."

"Great." She eyed my cheesecake. "Can I have a bite of your dessert? I'm running the New York City marathon tomorrow." Now this was a woman who knew what she wanted.

My new job started in October, and Mary Pat lived up to expectations—she was an amazing manager. The sales team consisted of several attractive and intelligent women. We would come up with some very creative marketing and sales ideas and then present them to Mary Pat. Her only comment became her signature line: "What's stopping ya?" When discussing finances, Mary Pat would pepper us with questions. Whom had we asked in the company for money? Why had that person said no? What was stopping him or her? By the end of the conversation, we all knew the only things holding us back were our own self-imposed limitations. Our sales team soon became unstoppable. The business at the account was increasing. In the midst of the busiest time of the year, I left and started at the hospital. The entire team divided up my responsibilities and agreed to cover for me. They even said they would pray for me. Whatever that means, I thought at the time.

# Chapter Three

My plan was to visit a young man I had seen pacing the hallways. I left Ted's office and went back up the stairs to the oncology floor. I found him sitting on a bench near the elevators next to a heavy woman. The census said he was twenty-three, but he looked fifteen. He was tall, at least five foot ten but very thin. His arms and legs were like sticks and seemed too long for his body. A baseball cap covered his hair and shaded most of his acne-scarred face. He sat on a pillow, covered with army camouflage fabric, to cushion his skinny body. At that moment, he was rummaging through a leather pouch. According to the census, his name was Charlie, and his diagnosis was testicular cancer.

"Hey, you," the heavy woman called. "Aren't you the chaplain?"

I hesitated, now that I had seen the two of them together, I was reluctant to talk to him. "Was there something that you needed?"

"Yeah, my son wants to go outside, and I'm too tired to take him out. He needs a wheelchair."

"Oh. Give me a minute. I saw one near the stairs." I hustled off to get it.

It took both of us to get Charlie into the wheelchair. His arms felt like cloth-covered bones, and his legs looked like disconnected pins stuck onto his body. His body flopped around like a rag doll. A heavy sigh escaped his lips as we lowered him into the chair.

"Just want … to sit … feel the warmth of the sun."

He pointed outside, and we headed toward the little courtyard a short distance down the hall. I guided his wheelchair over to a bench and sat next to him. He reached into the leather pouch and took out a cigarette and a lighter and smiled at me. He was missing a few teeth, and the ones he had left were discolored.

"Want a smoke?"

"No thanks, I don't smoke."

"Well, what's your gig in this place, or are you just hanging out waitin' on somebody?" He started blowing smoke rings.

"Not exactly. I'm here to help people with their spiritual needs." He closed his eyes and was quiet. His chest visibly moved with every breath.

"I'm having surgery tomorrow." He opened his eyes and looked at me. "They're going to remove my testicles. That's where the cancer started." He waited. "And now it's starting to spread."

The sun was hot for May. There was rain in the air. The entire atmosphere felt heavy and oppressive. Sweat was forming on my body, and I just wanted to get up and run back into the hospital. But I didn't. I stayed seated.

"I'm only twenty-three." The cigarette dropped from his fingers and laid smoking on the ground. We watched as the smoke gradually curled up and away. I thought about stepping on it, but we both watched in silence until the cigarette went out. Then I got up and took him back to his room.

I got a call about five that evening, asking for help with Charlie. He'd barricaded the door with his bed and one of those large, heavy recliners indigenous to hospital rooms.

The charge nurse ran her fingers through her hair and motioned toward the door. "He won't let us in the room. It's time for us to give him his meds to prep him for his surgery tomorrow. I called his mother at home, and she told me to call you."

"Really!" I stood on my tiptoes and peered through the window on the door to his room, and I could see Charlie sitting in the corner on the floor. The door moved slightly when I pushed on it. With the charge nurse's help, we pushed the door open enough for me to slip inside.

"Give us a little time," I said over my shoulder as I climbed over the bed and the chair.

"Charlie?" He didn't move. I picked up his pillow and sat down next to him on the floor. He took the pillow and hugged it to his chest. The two of us just sat there in silence. Time seemed to stop.

"Charlie?" We both looked up. The nurse was inching her way into the room with a glass of water and a cup of pills. "It's time." She bent down, handed him the glass, and spilled the pills into his hands. He took them all at once, and then we watched the nurse maneuver her way out of the room.

Charlie looked at me. "I can't see God. But I know he's really there. I know it now." I should have questioned why he now believed that God was really there, but instead, I sat there in silence, missing a golden opportunity to help Charlie and probably myself in the process.

He struggled to get up. I helped him, and he leaned on me as we walked over to his bed. I covered him up and held his hand until he closed his eyes and fell asleep.

# Chapter Four

Ted was sitting in his office, methodically spooning soup into his mouth. Once a week, at lunchtime, I would arrive in his office and spill my guts about what was going on during my chaplaincy. The chaplains were also required to submit a journal every week detailing their experiences, their feelings, and their theological reflections. Ted read the journals and wrote comments in the margins. Today, there was no question about how I was feeling. I was angry. Every muscle was tense like an over-stretched bungee cord; I sat on the edge of the chair, clutching the arms so fiercely that my fingernails had turned white.

"This is craziness, this job," I said through clenched teeth. He continued eating. "Yesterday, I spent an hour sitting on the floor of this kid's room doing nothing. I tried to pray, but it just seemed so hopeless. There was nothing I could do for him." I raised my voice for emphasis. "All I could do was sit next to him."

No reaction from Ted. He appeared to be entranced by the sound of his clock as it ticked away the seconds. Instead of hanging on the wall, this battery-operated wonder from China was sitting on top of one of the piles of papers, magazines, books, and folders. I could feel my body temperature rising, my eyes wandering over to titles on his bookshelf: *Addiction and Grace, Death and Dying, Basic Types of Pastoral Care.*

"Is this the kid with the testicular cancer?" he asked, setting down the soup bowl and starting in on his salad.

"Yes."

"So, what was it like for you to sit with that kid?"

"What was it like?" Was he kidding? "It was brutal. I never felt more helpless in my life. He's only twenty-three! He's a skeleton for heaven's sake. Praying for him seems ludicrous. I mean, what am I supposed to pray for?"

"So, you felt helpless. Probably not the feeling you're used to in your corporate life."

"Of course not, I'm paid to solve problems." My stomach muscles continued to tighten. I did not want to have this conversation. Ted should be focused on this poor kid who was probably waking up in recovery right this very moment, maimed forever. He would never be able to have children. Something needed to be *done*.

"And you couldn't fix this problem." He had set his salad down on the bookshelf and was leaning toward me.

"Right." Wasn't that obvious? Wasn't he listening?

"So, what *did* you do?"

"I sat with him."

"And what was that like?"

"I told you!" I hissed. "It was gut wrenching."

Speaking softly, Ted asked, "And what was it like for him?"

"I don't know. How could I know? I'm not twenty-three and dying." Tears started. I could feel them in the corners of my eyes. I was not in the mood to cry in front of this person at this moment.

"Well, you wrote in your journal that he said he couldn't see God but that he knew God was there."

"Yeah, so?"

Ted leaned back and put his hands behind his head. He stared at me for a moment. "So, how do you think he knows God is there?"

"I have no idea." My eyes felt big in my head, my body was on high alert, and all I wanted to do was stop this painful conversation.

Now it was Ted's turn to get frustrated. Although I noticed he seemed to control it. He took a deep breath.

"You sat with him, and you are the chaplain."

"But I'm not *God*."

Ted laughed. "No, you're not God, but you get to be present to people in the name of God. People appreciate that kind of *presence*, especially when they're ill."

"Really."

"Yes, Really. Why don't you go up and see how he made it through the surgery?

On the climb up eight flights of stairs, I struggled. How do I wrap my mind around not being able to do anything for patients? At one point in my life, I had thought about being a doctor. At least they could do something. I understood what Ted had said about "being there" with someone, but it seemed like a cop-out. For me, doing anything, executing a strategy, solving a problem, taking action, was primary.

Charlie was in intensive care. He was wearing an oxygen mask, and there were multiple bags of drugs attached to an IV pole. A technician was having trouble with the blood pressure cuff. It was just too big for his skinny arm. A nurse walked in and said, "Get a cuff from the pediatric ward." She glanced at my ID. "He needs prayers, this one." She shook her head.

I sat in the chair next to the bed. He needs prayers, so I should pray. Okay. God, this is awful. This kid is young, and his body is failing. What are you doing about it? What about all those miracles? Where are they now? Look at him. This felt like chatter in my head rather than a prayer, but it was all I could manage.

I turned when I heard Charlie's mother walk slowly into the room. She was carrying his army pillow and baseball cap. I got up from the chair, and she immediately sat down.

"Oh, honey, I'm so glad you're here with Charlie. It's like having God watchin' over him. It's like God is right here. Yup, yesterday Charlie told me about you settin' with him. You just sat there and didn't talk. He said it was what it must be like to be with God. He said God would just be with him and not tell him it was going to be all right, because it's not. He's dying, and he knows it. He just wants to know that God is with him. That's what you did." She was crying softly. "He wanted to be a soldier. He was willing to die for his country, but now he's dying because of the cancer. It's a battle he can't win. You go now, my dear, and be with other people. I'll stay with Charlie."

I turned to leave.

"And, honey?"

"Yes?"

"God bless you."

I made it to the ladies room before I started to cry.

## Chapter Five

Tonight was my first night on call. The CPE program required that the chaplains take turns staffing the hospital at night. The person on call would have the pager for thirty-six hours and respond to any emergency that occurred. On quiet nights, the chaplain was able to sleep in the on-call room. Other nights, the chaplain never slept.

I was waiting for Nick in the cafeteria. He was just coming off his thirty-six hour shift and was supposed to show me the ropes. I saw him enter the cafeteria, carrying his Bible and the pager, his eyes scanning the room.

"Nick!" I waved him over.

"Well, Julie. I will pray for you tonight. If it's anything like last night, you will need prayers. Trust me, it can get crazy." He sat down in the chair across from me. He was eating a Dove Bar.

"Is that dinner?" I asked, pointing at the ice cream that was beginning to drip onto his hand.

"Well, more like a reward." He slurped the creamy treat off the back of his hand. "I have one a day when I get done with my shift. So, how's the study on prayer coming?"

Great. Here it comes. He wants to convince me about prayer, and I was in no mood to argue with him. I was thinking too much about what could possibly happen in the middle of the night in a hospital where the very capable medical staff would feel the need to call a chaplain.

"Nick, show me the on-call room and how to work the pager."
I stood up and put my overnight bag on my shoulder.

"You probably won't be needing that!" He laughed. "I never even got to bed last night."

"Whatever, at least show me where I can put it."

The on-call room was tiny. Located on the seventh floor in a back hallway, there were no windows, the walls were concrete blocks, and the room looked more like a storage container for a small bed, a desk, and a chair. I dropped my stuff on the bed. The thought of spending time in this room almost made me wish that I might be busy during my shift.

"Now, you need to change the linens tomorrow when you get up, and ..." Nick pattered on, and then the next thing I knew, I had the pager. Nick grabbed my hands and said, "Let's pray." He was immediately off to that prayer place where the cadences of Lord, Lord were almost musical, if I could only relax and listen.

"Lord, you keep Julie in your hand, the hand that blesses, Lord, the hand that keeps us all safe, the hand that gives us new life, the hand that reaches out ...

Suddenly, I experienced an answered prayer. The pager went off, and Nick mercifully had to stop.

The emergency room was in full swing. Every chair was filled and people stood, leaned against the walls, and sprawled out all over the floor. I stepped over legs, pocketbooks, empty soda cans, a rag doll, and a baby's bottle as I made my way to the admittance desk. Fortunately, one of the admitting clerks saw me and was able to read my badge. "In there." She pointed to the trauma center and pressed a button. The doors opened.

It was like being transported into another world. Behind the curtained off areas and among the cacophony of sounds, I could distinguish voices calling for drugs, instruments, and compressions. The smell was almost sweet but metallic at the same time like fresh, wet soil. I had no idea what it was until I looked down. Fresh blood. There was a man with a bucket and mop working on the spill. I asked, "Did somebody page a chaplain?" He pointed toward a bed in the corner of the trauma center. There was something in the bed that looked like a person, but I couldn't tell if he or she was alive or dead. The person or body was motionless, and the eyes were closed. I sidestepped the blood and walked toward the bed.

The man looked like a wax dummy. It was like his face was totally devoid of blood. Surely he was dead. I looked back toward the man with the mop, but he had disappeared.

"Who are you?" My wax dummy had spoken.

"I'm the chaplain. Did you request a chaplain?"

"Really! I told them I was Catholic. And they send me a girl."

Girl, give me a break. At forty, I hardly considered myself a girl.

"Look, Mr. ..." I picked up his wrist and looked at his hospital bracelet, "Tozzo. I can page a Roman Catholic priest for you, but it could take a few hours."

"He doesn't have that kind of time." An emergency room nurse had entered the small area. "We're about to prep him for surgery. You have ten minutes."

"What can I do for you, Mr. Tozzo?"

He looked away.

Fine, this "girl" was leaving.

"Wait! I need to make a confession."

"Ok, what is it that you want to confess?"

He hesitated. "I don't want to say."

The nurse came back. "Are you done? We need to get him up to surgery."

Mr. Tozzo was squirming under the covers. "Just give us five minutes." He waited for the nurse to leave and then grabbed my arm. His grip was surprisingly strong. "Listen, I don't want to tell you what I did wrong, but I can't go to surgery without making a confession."

Now, here was a problem. "Okay, just think what you did wrong, and God will know it. God is the one who forgives sins." Now I was off the hook.

"Okay." He squeezed his eyes shut. "But will you say a prayer?"

"Sure. Gracious God, please forgive this man. Amen."

He opened his eyes, and I could see the lines of his face grow fainter as he relaxed. The difference in his entire demeanor was obvious. Even the color of his skin had changed like a spigot had been opened and newly oxygenated blood was running through his veins. The transport team was making its way through the trauma room to get his bed. I had no idea what had just happened.

On my way out of the trauma center, I heard the admittance desk call for Mrs. Tozzo. I waited to get a glimpse of his wife. Three women got up from the line of chairs and made their way to the admittance desk. Simultaneously, they chorused "I'm Mrs. Tozzo." Three wives! The women stared at each other. And then my pager went off.

My pager was calling me to the eighth floor. As I climbed the stairs, I wondered if God had truly forgiven this man. Somehow, I didn't think New York State would be as forgiving—or the women! It was no wonder the guy had heart problems. What had amazed me was how quickly he had relaxed after the short prayer. I had once heard that the feeling of forgiveness is like taking a warm shower, but instead of water, it's love that is being poured out. A love that helps begin some kind of healing process.

I reached the eighth floor and announced myself to the nurse's station. The woman behind the desk looked up at me and said, "We have a situation."

"What kind of situation?" I couldn't begin to imagine.

"A family situation."

My mind immediately went to a possible car accident with multiple victims. They were probably all here in intensive care. How awful.

"Room twenty-four." The woman had gotten up and was leaving.

"Who's in room twenty-four?"

"The mother."

This was getting worse. I pictured myself going from room to room, keeping the family updated on each other's progress. Hopefully, not having to bring bad news. I walked into the mother's room. It was crowded with people. I squeezed past two young couples—both of the women were clutching the arms of their men—so I could see who was in the bed. I found myself looking at a woman who was probably five feet tall and one hundred pounds soaking wet. She was hooked up to two IV poles, one on each side. Multiple bags hung from them like huge bunches of grapes at harvest time, and the cardiac monitor beeped away above the bed. Whatever was going on, she certainly did not look like the victim of a car accident.

"And who are you?" A younger version of the woman in the bed had walked up to me and stood about two inches from my face.

"I'm the chaplain on call," I said, lifting my ID badge so it was eye level.

"She's *not* dying," the woman screeched. "We do *not* need a chaplain."

"Okay. Maybe I'm in the wrong room. Is this room twenty-four?"

"Yes, this is room twenty-four, my mother's room. She's sick, but she's going to get better." The woman maneuvered herself to the side of the hospital bed and bent down close to her mother's ear. "You're getting better, right, Mom? You will be going home soon. Just a few more days." The woman's jaw was set, and her eyes stared down at her mother, almost willing her to get up and speak.

The woman in the bed did not respond.

"Alice, you should let her rest." A tall middle-aged man got out of the chair next to the bed and put his arms around Alice. She shrugged them off.

"I know what she needs. You are going to get better, Mom." She turned and looked right at me. "She is getting better." She stood with her arms folded across her chest, her legs shoulder width apart and her mouth set in a firm line, daring me to say otherwise.

"Well," I said, "why don't we say a prayer for your mother."

"Sure! That would be great. We can pray for her recovery." Alice came over to me and took my hand. "First, let me introduce you to my family. This is my husband, Stuart." I shook hands with the tall middle-aged man. This is my cousin Sally and her husband, Dave, and this is my brother Al and his wife, Lisa, and this is …" And around the room we went.

I now understood "family situation." I naively wondered what the entire family was doing here. As the thought crossed my mind, a nurse entered the room. She had a big red heart on her ID badge, and she was dressed in pink pastel scrubs. Her hair surrounded her face in a halo of brown curls. She smiled at the group and quietly said, "I'm looking for Alice?"

"I'm Alice." She let go of my hand, walked over to the side of the bed, and picked up her mother's hand. "What do you want?" Her voice sounded like a guard dog that had just heard a rustle in the woods.

"Your mother's doctor has asked me to talk to you about placing your mother on comfort care."

"I've already discussed this with him, and I said no. I don't want you giving up on my mother. She's going to get better." Alice barked out these orders like a drill sergeant, her body between the nurse and the bed. Then she turned, bent over, and placed her mouth right next to her mother's ear. "Right, Mom? "You are getting better, and you will be going home. Don't worry, Mom, I will get you whatever you need to get better." She straightened up and looked at the nurse. "We do not need your kind of care. We have the chaplain here, and she was just about to pray for Mom's recovery."

The nurse sent me an incredulous look. "Recovery?"

"I just got paged here," I said. Too late, the nurse was already rolling her eyes. She threw me a bone as she walked out of the room. "You must be new," she said under her breath.

Alice gathered the family around the bed for "the prayer." I groaned inwardly. What was I supposed to say? "Dear God," I began. *Help!* "Show this woman your merciful and loving presence, and heal her from all her afflictions."

When I finished, I practically ran for the door. "I must go." I lifted up the pager. "I'm being paged."

The comfort-care nurse was waiting in the hall. "What are you doing in there? Giving them false hope? That woman is actively dying."

"First of all, I'm not a doctor. I had no idea the woman was dying, and I'm not in there giving false hope. I'm just praying with the family."

"Well, you must be new. You need to check with the charge nurse before you go barging into any situation. You need to know what's going on before you enter a room. In that room, we have a daughter who is in total denial that her mother is dying. All of her organs are failing, and it's really only a matter of days. The idea would be to make her comfortable and stop all these unnecessary treatments. We can't get the daughter to let go of the hope that her mother is going to get better and go home! We paged you to help us with that."

"All I heard was that we had a family situation. I had no idea what was going on."

"Well, now you know." She turned around and walked down the hall while I stood outside the room wondering what I should do. Cousin Dave walked out.

"Hey, any idea where I could go for a smoke?"

"Yeah sure, just take the elevator to the ground floor. There's a courtyard where you can smoke."

"Ya know, Alice is a little bit of a nut case. She'll be screaming at the grave when her mother is dead and buried that she is going to get better any minute and go home. She's quite attached to her mother." He squinted at me, and his head tilted as his hands searched his pockets for his cigarettes.

"Well, I could tell that she seemed quite concerned." He smiled at me and took off in the direction of the elevators.

The doors to the room opened again, and the rest of the family started coming out. "We're on our way home now," one of the women told me. "We live about fifty miles away."

"What about Alice?"

"Oh no, she stays the night."

"Every night?"

"Every night."

The door was cracked. I could see Alice moving around getting ready to settle into the chair next to her mother's bed. It was nine o'clock. I headed to the on-call room.

# Chapter Six

The on-call room was pitch black. I put my hand in front of my face and opened my eyes. I couldn't see a thing. My mind wouldn't shut off to let me sleep. What was I doing here? Two weeks ago I was selling computers. My sales team had taken me to dinner in Los Angeles. They had been very supportive of my ordination process and had offered to cover for me during the three months I had planned to be gone. "We will be praying for you," they said.

Andrea, another sales rep, was the most curious about what she called "my journey." Before I left LA, we had decided to have drinks—just the two of us. She was fascinated by a denomination that encouraged women to be clergy. We had both grown up Roman Catholic, and neither one of us could imagine a woman being ordained to the priesthood. Andrea was Irish Catholic. Her stories about her childhood religion were more intense than my German Catholic upbringing. Today, the only part of her Irish heritage that Andrea claimed was her freckles. The rest of Andrea was pure southern California. For our dinner, Andrea had chosen a dark-blue, size two Ann Taylor suit. Her hair was perfectly cut, her nails were manicured with a pale pink polish, and her perfectly tanned legs were finished off with strappy designer sandals. We had decided to stay out late after the team dinner.

"So, what do they call you?" Andrea asked and took a sip of wine. We were sitting in dark—red leather chairs around a low table in her favorite wine bar. I watched the waves of the Pacific through the picture window roll away, leaving shells and seaweed on the beach.

"Julie, I would imagine." I hadn't even gotten to this issue in my own thought process about becoming a priest. "In the Episcopal church, a lot of the men go by Father and some of the women use Mother, but I think I will go with Julie."

"And this hospital chaplaincy is the last thing you have to do before you get ordained?"

"No, there are still a few more hurdles to jump." I reached for the bottle of wine and refilled my glass. Thinking about all the requirements of ordination was overwhelming.

"For heaven's sake, Julie, you have a great job and a wonderful life; why on earth are you going through this? What made you want to be ordained?"

"Would you believe a bad sales call?"

She laughed but stopped when she saw I was serious. "You're not kidding. There has got to be more to the story than a bad sales call."

"Oh, I guess there is."

She ordered another bottle of wine. "Let's hear it."

"Well, as you know, I grew up Roman Catholic. My parents did not attend church regularly, but they made us go to catechism every Tuesday night. I remember making my first communion, and then as I got older, my mom took us to confirmation classes. When she picked us up, one of the nuns came out and asked her why we never came to church. We rarely went because we were rarely home. Our family went skiing or hiking on the weekends. After I made my confirmation, that was it. No more church, no more classes. I didn't go back until after I had my first child."

The wine arrived, and I paused while the waitress went through the tasting ritual with Andrea. Andrea was very fussy about her wines. She didn't eat much, but she certainly could put away the wine.

"Can you bring us an appetizer menu?" Unlike Andrea, I had to eat something in order to keep from getting too drunk.

Andrea nodded her approval, and the waitress poured the wine. "So, what year was your first child born?"

"Eighty-three. I had a very hard time getting pregnant with him. I finally took a fertility drug that worked. I felt like I needed to thank God for having a child, and I also felt compelled to have him baptized. I was taught as a child that an unbaptized person would go to hell. I didn't really believe it, but the thought was there, so I went church shopping."

"Why didn't you go back to the Roman Catholic Church?"

"Birth control."

"Birth control?" Andrea's voice was getting louder with each sip of wine.

"Yeah, I knew I would be using birth control."

"For goodness sake, Julie, everyone uses birth control," she said too loudly. We started to get some looks.

"I know, but the church says no birth control."

She shrugged and rolled her eyes. "Okay, so—"

"I ended up in the Episcopal church. They were just beginning to ordain women, they didn't prohibit birth control, and their Sunday liturgy was more like what I remembered from the few times I had attended church."

"So, how did you go from baptizing a baby to preparing for ordination?"

The waitress arrived with some chicken wings and set them on the table. "These are from that table over there. They thought you could use some food."

We looked at each other and laughed. Andrea took one and began her dissection process. She took a small piece of meat with her fingers and put it in her mouth.

"Well, after my son was baptized, I quit going to church. Then I had another son. I got him baptized and then quit going to church. When my third son was born, I got him baptized and—"

"Let me guess, you quit going to church? I sense a pattern." She was still chewing her first bite.

I finished my first wing and started another. "After that I quit having babies, and I quit going to church. I quit until this priest showed up on my doorstep one day. I saw her coming up the walk. I tried to hide, but she saw me through the window. I had to let her in."

"So, she got you back to church."

"Yeah, for a little while."

"I would just come for a little while and then leave. I didn't feel that religious. I believed in God, but I wasn't sure about Jesus. It was hard with three kids, and I was having marital problems."

Andrea was now halfway done with the chicken wing, but she was pouring the last little bit of wine in her glass from the bottle we had just ordered.

"Okay," she said. You had a roller-coaster church ride. Cut to the bottom line. Get to the sales call."

"I went to look at some defective hardware at this company. They wanted me to take it all back. It was stored in a locked room in their warehouse. When the man who called me to look at it opened the door, the room was filled with pornography. It was everywhere. I looked at him, and I could see that he was waiting for my reaction. I told him we would take it all back right that second and that I was going to call the purchasing manager at his company to come down and take inventory with me. His face turned white, and he started stammering that maybe he was being too hard on me by asking me to take back these printers. I was already heading to a phone."

"This is your call to the priesthood?"

"It was actually what happened after that experience. He insisted that it was all a mistake, and I left. I drove around the city letting off a little steam. What a waste of my time. I mean, the guy was nuts. He was trying to intimidate me. As I was driving, I saw a bunch of beautiful brick buildings, so I drove onto the grounds. I went inside and asked the receptionist where I was. She told me I was at a school. So I asked her for a class schedule. It was January, it was gray, it was cold, I was getting divorced, I was depressed, and I needed something. I signed up for a class called "St. Paul and other writings." She told me it would cost one thousand twenty-one dollars. I was a little shocked, but I was beginning to feel desperate. I wanted something different. My checkbook balance was one thousand twenty-one dollars. I wrote the check."

Andrea just stared at me. The half-eaten chicken wing lay on her plate next to the empty wine glass.

"I went to the first class and the professor said, 'Pull out your Bibles.' I didn't have a Bible. I didn't realize it was a Bible class. While people were getting their Bibles, he had us introduce ourselves. I quickly realized that everyone was studying for the ministry. When they got to me, I said I didn't know what I was doing there, and everyone laughed. Apparently they knew I would come around and recognize my calling. I'm still unsure about all of this, but every time I take a class or complete another requirement, it seems right." I stood up.

Andrea wiped her fingers on a Wet-Nap and came around the table to hug me. "You go, girl," she whispered. "It is right."

# Chapter Seven

As I laid there in the on-call bed, I thought I would have given anything for a glass of wine. Maybe it would help to shut off my brain. This chaplaincy experience was not what I expected. When had they told us about staying overnight? Here I was ten miles away from my own house, away from my husband and kids, lying in what felt like a concrete cell, and waiting for morning.

Next thing I knew, I was hearing musical notes going up and down the scale. What the was that? I sat up. Where am I? I couldn't see. The notes continued as my eyes scanned the blackness. Green numbers were flashing on the bedside table. The pager had gone off.

Since I hadn't bothered to undress, I got up quickly and punched the numbers into a phone in the hallway. An electronic voice answered, "Emergency page." No kidding, I thought, this information was not helpful. The last few times I had called the number on the pager, I had gotten a live person. I made my way down the stairs to the main lobby.

A security guard slumped at the desk. He was reading the paper and sipping a steaming hot cup of coffee. I eyed the coffee. Where did he get that? It was 3:00 a.m., and the coffee counter had been closed since eight.

"Uh, excuse me," I said. "What is an emergency page?"

He slowly moved his eyes up the paper and squinted at my ID badge. After he finished perusing my badge, he went back to reading his paper.

I stood there and contemplated my next move. At this point the pager went off again.

"Lady, you might want to try emergency."

"Oh. Thanks!"

The emergency room waiting area looked the same as it had at the beginning of my shift. There were wall-to-wall people, except this time some of them were sound asleep in their chairs. I stepped around a few bodies snoring on the floor as I made my way to the admitting clerk. This time she recognized me and buzzed me in to the trauma center.

A group of people encased in blue scrubs and yellow gowns surrounded a table. They looked like a football team huddling before the major play of the game, except everyone was moving. Arms were flying, and torsos were moving back and forth on top of what looked like a body of a very tall and broad man. Another blur of blue scrubs entered the trauma center. This man was wearing a surgical mask around his neck. He glanced over his shoulder at me on his way into the huddle. "Your job is to pray that we save this guy," he said. The group parted to let him through.

Uh huh, I thought, this must be the quarterback. I started praying immediately. "Please, God," I murmured, "please let this one live." I stood there for I don't know how long and repeated this prayer over and over. The team was relentless. IVs were started, shots were given, compressions were done, and a respirator was hooked up, but none of it mattered. It didn't work. The man died.

"Time of death," the doctor quarterback said, "is 5:30 a.m." The activity ceased, and for a moment, there was silence in the trauma room.

"Chaplain?" The doctor was looking at me. "Would you please say a prayer?"

My brain froze. For what, I thought; the man was dead. I walked toward the body as the blue scrubs parted for me. It was the first time I had really seen the man. He was bare-chested and appeared to be wearing a bathing suit. The respirator tube was still in his mouth, but his chest was still. I picked up his hand. It was cold and clammy. I stared at his face. It was weather beaten and wrinkled but looked kind. His laugh lines were deep. It was an in-between moment. I could see the signs of life that had been there just a moment before, and I was also aware of the very present signs of death. He was a body without breath. A shell. I felt a calmness and peace wash over me.

"Holy One" I began. The entire team and the doctor bowed their heads. "Accept this your servant into your loving arms; help his family in their grief; and give these people here, who tried to save this man, the strength and courage to continue to save those who can be saved. Amen." There was a collective sigh from the group. Then people began to collect hardware and the inevitable detritus that comes from opening sterile equipment and disposable medical products. I sat down in a chair. I didn't know what to think or feel or do. The peace was gone. I just felt utterly exhausted.

I felt a hand on my shoulder. It was Doctor Quarterback. "Thank you for responding to the page and for praying. It makes a huge difference to me to have someone praying in the room at a time like this."

This was a surprise. I heard what he was saying, but I didn't know what it meant. All I could think of was that the guy died. Wasn't that the wrong outcome? Shouldn't the prayer help the person on the table?

"He's something isn't he?" An older woman from the huddle of blue scrubs had taken a seat next to me. "He's a very religious doctor. He likes to feel God's presence at a death. Prayer helps him connect to God and to the person. Having a human presence praying for us really helps. This job can get quite discouraging. Thank you." She smiled. "You had better prepare yourself."

"For what?" I couldn't imagine.

She looked puzzled. "For telling the family. He just went to change his scrubs, and then he'll be back. He'll want you to go with him to tell the family."

"Oh." I wondered which set of people in the waiting room was his family.

They weren't in the main waiting room. They were seated in the family waiting room. I quickly came to understand that when people were placed in the private family waiting room, this meant the family member was critical. It was a small windowless room with chairs and a love seat. There were Kleenex boxes on the end tables. I edged in the door and saw a man and a woman sitting on the love seat holding hands. They looked like they were in their fifties. A younger man, around twenty, stood nervously next to the older couple. The woman's eyes searched our faces for news. The doctor closed the door and sat down. He introduced me to the woman, and when she heard the word chaplain, I saw the first flicker of fear cross her face.

"We did everything we could," he began and then proceeded to describe all the medical intervention the team had done to try and save what I soon learned was their father's and grandfather's life. "I'm sorry," the doctor continued, "but he died at 5:30 a.m. Do you have any questions?" There was a long pause. The woman looked at the doctor.

"Thank you," she said and began to cry softly.

"The chaplain can take you in to see him when you're ready. I'm really sorry." The doctor left.

I sat down in the chair vacated by the doctor. "What happened?" In my short time at the hospital, I had learned that people got some comfort by telling their story.

There was silence. The woman continued to cry, and the younger man looked uncomfortable. Finally, the twenty-something volunteered, "He was windsurfing."

"At night?" I couldn't help myself. It just came out. Who windsurfs at night, especially at eighty-three? I had looked up his age on his chart while I was waiting for the doctor.

The woman cried harder. The older man patted her back and said, "He had a heart condition, but he loved to windsurf. His doctor had told him he needed to give it up. He was always going out windsurfing by himself, and we were all afraid he would have a heart attack and drown. Last night, he snuck down to the dock around midnight to go windsurfing. This one here saw him go down there in his bathing suit and did nothing to stop him." He was pointing at the young man.

"He wanted to go! He wanted to do the only thing he really loved doing. You guys took that away from him." He was on his feet pointing at the couple.

I stood up and touched his arm. "It's okay; sit down and tell me what else happened."

The young man slowly sat down and put his head in his hands. The older man continued. "Mark followed him down to the dock in time to see him get on the board and paddle out into the lake. There wasn't much wind, but there was enough to keep the sail up. He watched Fred sail for a few minutes, and then Fred dropped the sail and sat down on the board, clutching his heart. By the time Mark had alerted us, called an ambulance, and then got a boat out to get Fred, he was in bad shape. The EMT crew had to get him up a long set of steep stairs that go from the lake to the house and then into the ambulance. It took forever to get him here, and by that time, there wasn't much left to do."

"It sounds like he died doing something he really loved to do." The three of them just stared at me. I suddenly realized that *how* he died didn't change the fact that he had died.

"Can we see him now?" the woman asked.

I led the family into the trauma room. Fred's body was on the stretcher, still in his swim trunks and the breathing tube still down his throat. The friendly nurse was picking up the trash that had been thrown around the room.

"Oh, Daddy, I'm so sorry." The woman bent over his body and hugged his chest. "I should have never taken away your windsurfer board." The two men put their arms around her, and the family held each other and cried.

I stepped outside the curtain. The nurse looked at me and smiled. She whispered, "Some people are just going to go ahead and die the way they want. He died doing what he loved. God bless him for it." I nodded. It was seven thirty in the morning. It was time for the on-call chaplain report.

I walked slowly up one flight of stairs from the emergency room to the chaplain's office. The group was gathered around the mailboxes, looking over the lists of patients on their assigned units.

"So, how was it?" Beth asked. She hadn't done an overnight shift yet.

"Busy." I got myself a cup of coffee. I didn't want to tell my story twice. All I could think of was getting through the report and then going home and going to bed. I was exhausted. I couldn't remember the last time I had pulled an all-nighter. Probably college.

Ted called the group to order. Frank, typically late to these meetings, snuck in during our opening prayer. Every morning the chaplains got together, listened to the on-call report, and reviewed any issues that might have come up for a member of the group. On two mornings a week, when the group then stayed for a "didactic," a teaching session on pastoral care by one of the staff, Frank always looked bored. Well, he wouldn't be bored this morning.

"Okay, Julie, let's hear what happened last night." Ted sat back, and I launched into my stories of the man with the three wives; the dying woman who wasn't dying, according to her daughter; and the windsurfing grandfather.

"Wow," Beth said under her breath, "you just can't make this stuff up."

"No kidding," I said. I hadn't even begun to process what had happened the night before. A man had died in front of me. I was just beginning to realize what I had seen.

"So, Julie, how are you doing with all of this?" Ted was watching me. I'm sure I looked a little dazed.

"Okay, I guess. I feel a little numb. There was a lot happening."

"Is there anything you would like to talk about with the group?"

"Not really." I was beginning to feel uncomfortable. Was I supposed to be talking about something?

"Well, I'm wondering what it was like for you to watch someone die." Ted sat back and waited.

He wasn't going to let it go. Couldn't he see that all I wanted to do was get out of there? I had been working for twenty-four hours in a row. Sleep was all I wanted.

"He was eighty-three," I said defensively.

"Yes." Ted waited.

"He died doing something he loved!"

Silence filled the room while everyone waited. What did they want me to say? All of a sudden, I could feel myself crack like the shell of a soft-boiled egg. The night's drama played itself through my head, and my emotions leaked out like a runny yolk.

"It's hard to watch people suffer." The group leaned in to hear what I had said. Someone handed me a tissue, and I realized that tears were streaming down my face.

"How crazy was that man with his wives; now what are they going to do? His life is a mess! And the daughter," I was letting the tears fall freely now, "she just wants her mother to live."

And then it hit me, I watched a man die, and I had to take his daughter and grandson in to say good-bye to him. Good-bye forever.

"And someone died. There was nothing I could do about it. Nothing."

"You had quite a night, Julie. There was a lot going on, and it is hard to watch people suffer." Ted came over and put his arm around my shoulders. "Remember, it's not your husband, your mother, or your grandfather. Seeing people in these situations can bring up our own feelings about the people in our own lives. We start thinking about what happens when our parents or grandparents die. We may even begin to contemplate our own death. We can talk more about that later. It's time to get up to the floors." He stopped himself. "Is there anyone who has an issue to bring before the group?"

Nick raised his hand.

"Yes, Nick, what can we help you with?"

"Well, I did an emergency baptism last night on the psych ward, and the nurses gave me a hard time about it."

Ted's head snapped around. "You did what?"

"I was walking out to my car after I had handed over the on-call pager to Julie. On my way I saw them bringing a patient into the psych ward. He was agitated, and the nurses were having trouble calming him down, so I offered to help." Nick was smiling, looking very pleased with himself.

"Nick, you should have paged Julie. She was the chaplain on call. It was after hours; if the nurses need a chaplain, they page one."

His smile wavered for a moment. "I did succeed in calming him down. He had tried to commit suicide, and he was being brought in on a mental health arrest. His neighbor called the cops when they saw him come out of his building with blood all over his wrists."

Ted's jaw muscles clenched. "So, how did this situation turn into a baptism?" he asked through his teeth.

"Uh, I uh suggested that he needed to be baptized."

"And why would you suggest this?"

"He said he hadn't been baptized, so I thought I would do it in case he died." Nick was beginning to fidget in his chair.

"Okay, let me see if I'm hearing you. A man comes in to the psych ward and he's agitated. The nurses can't calm him down. You find out that his neighbor made a mental health arrest and that the man had tried to kill himself by cutting his wrists, and your response to this situation is to find out if he had been baptized?"

"Yeah, almost. I calmed him down first."

"And was his condition life threatening?" Ted's face had gotten red, and the veins on his neck were clearly visible.

"Not exactly."

"So, what made you decided to do an emergency baptism?"

Nick was sweating. "We talked about what might make him feel better. I told him that Jesus was there for him, and he wanted to know how. So, I said that in baptism, we are united with Christ. Then he interrupted me and said that he didn't think he had ever been baptized. Then he asked me if I thought this would make him feel better and make some of the bad thoughts go away, and I said yes." Nick sat back and folded his arms across his chest.

The group looked at Ted. His face was back to normal. He sighed, took a long sip of his coffee, and looked around the room. "Any thoughts?"

Beth was already there. "How could you? How could you baptize someone who wasn't dying and obviously not in his right mind? Who do you think you are? And then you tell him that this would make him feel better?

Nick turned away from Beth. "You don't even believe in baptism. What do you know? Who do you think you are? You weren't there."

Ted looked around at the rest of the group. Frank looked bored, I was too tired to think, and Judy looked horrified.

"Nick, think about it," Judy said calmly. "First of all, he said he didn't know if he had been baptized. Instead of pursuing his spiritual and religious background, you just stepped in and baptized him with no investigation or instruction. Since he wasn't in any danger of dying and since he probably wasn't in a state of mind where he could make an informed decision about being baptized, I think you were dead wrong." Judy looked over at Ted who was nodding.

Nick was glowering at Judy and Beth.

"I did the right thing. He wanted to be baptized. He had almost died, so I baptized him." Nick voice was sounding a little squeaky.

"Well, Nick, I think you and I should take a walk over to the psych ward and see what your patient thinks this morning. It's time to get up to your units." Ted stood up.

I grabbed my coat and started for the door.

"Where are you going?" Ted asked.

"Home?"

"I don't think so; on-call is a thirty-six hour shift."

I stared at Ted's back as he and Nick left the office together. How could I go back up on the unit for another eight hours? I felt physically and emotionally drained. I couldn't imagine sitting and talking with one more patient. I headed for the coffee stand. I needed a large.

# Chapter Eight

The line for coffee was very long. I didn't care. It was a necessity. Frank got in line behind me.

"Hey, Julie, we should probably rename Nick 'John the Baptizer.' He's wanted to do a baptism since he got here." Frank laughed. "Nick told me that the senior pastor at his church wouldn't let him baptize. I knew it was just a matter of time."

"Oh, Frank, that's awful." I was shocked.

"Well, what can you do? Ted will help him out. He needs to recognize what issues are his and separate those out from the needs of the patient. We all do." He sighed. "It's so easy to get caught up in our own stuff. Being aware of our own wounds and our own desires are critical for the ministry."

"So, how do you do that?" I was thinking back over my limited experience, wondering if I was guilty of ignoring the needs of the patient in order to satisfy my own.

"You have to be aware of what is going on inside of you while you're with someone. You have to watch yourself." Frank motioned to the person in line behind us to go ahead. "I find that if I'm having an intense emotional reaction to something that isn't really about me, that's a red flag."

"What do you mean? Do you have an example?" We moved out of the coffee line.

"Well, think about the windsurfing grandfather." Frank was watching me carefully. "Do you have a grandfather?"

"Not anymore. They're both dead." I felt tears come to my eyes as I remembered my own grandfather dying in the hospital bed.

"That's it! You're thinking about your grandfather, right?"

"Yes, of course, you just asked me about him." Now I was confused.

"The trick is to remember that someone else's grandfather is not your grandfather. If you feel sad about a man you never knew, it's really coming from the grief that you feel about your own grandfather."

"Oh."

"You'll see." Frank guided me back into the coffee line.

\* \* \* \* \*

The hot coffee felt good in my hands and in some small way, comforting. The smell of hazelnut floated up to my noise. I inhaled deeply and started toward the stairs. Maybe I could find a patient's room where I could just sit, think, and start to process some of what had happened.

As I began the climb up the stairs, I heard loud and fast footsteps coming down. I flattened myself against the side of the stairwell to get out of the way. The person turned out to be a small, young-looking girl, dressed in scrubs, with a colorful teddy-bear top. Her eyes were focused on her feet, and it wasn't until she jumped the last two steps onto the landing that she saw me clutching my coffee protectively between my body and the wall.

"Whoa! Slow down," I said.

"I can't believe it!" She was staring at the small black Bible that I always carried. "You're a chaplain? I can't believe it." She had picked up my hospital ID that I wore constantly around my neck. She looked at it and then at me as if to verify that I truly belonged to the ID badge. Her face was flushed, and she looked like a kid that had just come in from playing a game of kickball. Her ID badge said Erin Murphy, LPN.

She grabbed my hand and started to pull me up the stairs. Some of my coffee sloshed out of the hole in the lid onto my hand.

"Whoa, just a minute, uh, Erin? Where are we going?"

"I was praying that I could find a chaplain, and I was running to the chaplain's office to get one, and here you are, and we need to go right now." She exhaled the entire sentence in one breath while continuing to pull me up the stairs. A trail of coffee stains followed.

"Erin!" Her name echoed in the stairwell. "What is this about?"

"The family needs you." She stopped long enough to look at me. Her eyes were green and wide like a declawed cat that had been cornered by dogs.

"Why does the family need me?"

"You just have to come." She grabbed my hand tighter and practically dragged me through the door to the fourth floor. The unit secretary watched us coming down the hall and picked up a four-ounce bottle of sterile water and handed it to me. It was a baby bottle without the nipple. Erin pulled me into a room where a young woman was lying in the bed.

"I'll be right back," she called over her shoulder as she left the room, closing the door behind her.

It was a large private room with comfortable chairs scattered around and a round table in the corner. It resembled a living room more than a hospital room. The woman in the bed kept her eyes closed.

"Hi, I'm the chaplain," I said as I moved closer.

She opened her eyes and started to cry. "Thank you for coming. It's been so hard, so hard. I'm so tired."

I pulled a tissue out of my pocket and handed it to her. She looked as young as the nurse. Her unusually pale face seemed even more so against her matted black hair. She looked like she'd just run marathon. She stopped crying and tried to pull herself up.

"Just rest," I said. My eyes settled on an empty crib on the other side of the room. She saw me looking at it and then the door opened.

Erin, carrying a small bundle, accompanied by another nurse, came back into the room.

"Here." She handed me the bundle, totally encased in a receiving blanket.

My heart nearly stopped. My hands immediately identified the shape of a baby. Erin gently lifted the blanket to expose the tiny face. The child couldn't have weighed more than four pounds. The eyes were closed, and the featherlike eyelashes were so long that they brushed the cheeks. The baby had a cute upturned nose and a rosebud mouth. The head was covered with tiny hairs. My first instinct was to coo over this beautiful and serene looking child. But as I held the child, the weight of the baby in my hands translated into the thought, dead weight. The baby was dead.

The mother and both nurses waited patiently as I examined the infant.

"I'm sorry," I said to the mother. She began to cry silently.

The older nurse opened the bottle of sterile water.

"Time for the baptism," she said.

Baptism? The baby was dead. When I had thought about the ministry, I had imagined my first baptism in a church with proud family members and a child in a beautiful white gown. It was all I could do to hold the baby. I had never seen death like this. My mind began racing with the theology I had learned growing up. Dead babies went to limbo. I knew that this theology was not what most people still believed, but it was all coming back to me. How could I baptize this baby? In seminary, I had learned that baptism was about entering into the community of Christ. Wasn't the baby already with God? I dragged my mind back into the present. The nurse was handing me the water.

"What's the child's name?" I asked.

"Mary Margaret Burns," the mother whispered.

I asked God to bless the water and then put some on my thumb. I placed my thumb on the baby's forehead to make the sign of the cross, and then everything seemed to stop. The skin of the baby was the softest thing I had ever touched. My thumb sank into the skin. Skin on skin, life on death, a beginning and ending all at the same time. I was flooded with warmth, and I recognized it as an intense feeling of love.

"I baptize Mary Margaret Burns in the name of the Father and of the Son and of the Holy Spirit. Amen."

The mother reached for the baby as I placed her into her mother's arms, and the crying began in earnest.

The coffee was cold, but I sipped it anyway as I continued my journey up the stairs like a sleepwalker. I was trying to process what had just happened.

As I entered the seventh-floor unit, the secretary said, "They want you in the chaplain's office."

"Did they say why?"

"Nope, just that you had to go there."

I took the elevator back down to the lobby level and walked quickly to the chaplain's office. At least there was a microwave in the office and the possibility of reheated coffee.

Diane was the chaplain's office secretary. She was everyone's mother in a pastoral sense. Many times I had walked by the office and seen one of the other chaplain interns standing next to her desk telling a story. Diane's face was always focused on the intern, eyes expressive, listening intently. The office phone would ring and Diane wouldn't even hear it. Whoever was talking to her became her entire world. She was a model of good listening.

Today, her face was full of sympathy. Had she already heard about the baby? "Julie, Judy is the chaplain on call, but she's tied up in the emergency room. I need to send you to another emergency. I left messages with all the unit secretaries to send me the first chaplain they saw, and you were the one who appeared."

I tried to listen to what Diane was telling me while my coffee heated up. I pulled out the now-steaming cup, and the smell of hazelnut brought back my morning thought: my desperate desire to go somewhere and just sit.

"One of the nurses in the chemo center was shot and killed last night." Diane pulled a chair over to the side of her desk. I sat down.

"It was a drive-by shooting. Apparently she was sitting on her front porch, waiting for her grandson to come home, and there was a fight going on in front of her house. Someone pulled up, took out a gun, and fired. She was hit and died on the way to the hospital. They need a chaplain to come up and do a prayer service. Her name was Elsie and everyone loved her. Everyone. They need you in the conference room of the chemo center at two. Julie, are you okay?"

"Yeah, I'm just not sure what to do."

"Well, I've heard you're studying prayer; why don't you just ask God what to do, and in case you need more help, there are prayer services in the top drawer of that file cabinet. I have to leave for lunch in a few minutes. I'll pray for you!"

Diane stood up and began cleaning up her desk. I looked over at the filing cabinet. "Please, God, help me figure out what to do." I uttered this over and over as I rifled through the files of prayer services.

Two hours later, I had managed to cut and paste some Scripture readings and prayers together and was on my way to the conference room. The windowless door was shut and hard to open because I was carrying papers and a Bible. Someone grabbed the door from the inside, and I tried to step into the room. "Who are you?" the person holding the door asked.

"The chaplain." She moved aside, and I saw at least fifty people cramped into a small conference room designed for twenty, most of them standing. Surprisingly, no one was talking. I stood there uncertain of where to go. The older woman seated at the head of the conference table stood up and moved aside. The rest of the staff made a path for me.

I stood at the head of the table, and for the first fifteen minutes, I prayed the prayers and read the scripture I had chosen. There was absolutely no response. The room had a heaviness that only a full-blown thunderstorm would relieve. I had run out of material. I threw in the Lord's Prayer. A few people weakly joined in. Please, God, help me know what to do, I thought. My two hours of preparation had been for nothing. This group was unresponsive.

I stopped and listened to the heavy silence. In a sudden realization, I knew that the silence was heavy because it was full of stories. This was the answer to my prayer. The sentence was loud in my head. Have them tell their stories about Elsie.

"At this time, I would like to invite you to share your stories about Elsie. When you feel ready, please feel free to speak." I sat back down and waited. A minute went by, then five minutes; I started to squirm. Now what? I wondered. I couldn't stand the silence, the faces of grief, and the limp bodies that showed only numbness and shock. At the ten-minute mark, I looked around the room, panic stricken. How do I end this? The older woman who had given me her place at the table was looking at me. I nodded to her, and she began to speak. At first she was hesitant, but then she warmed to her story.

"Elsie was always there." She paused and looked slowly around the room. "She was there for everybody."

A few people nodded. They were all listening intently.

"She covered my shifts for me when my brother was dying and I was doing hospice at my house. I found out later that she was working her own shift from seven to three and then working my three to eleven shifts. She did two shifts a day for two weeks just to help me out."

The woman paused again. We watched her tears slowly make their way down her cheeks like rain on a window.

"I remember those two weeks. There was always a basket with food on my doorstep. I didn't know where the food was coming from until my son told me he had heard a noise at five thirty in the morning. When he looked out the window, he saw Elsie getting out of her car with the food basket. She was dropping it off on her way to work. If she was working two shifts, when did she have time to cook?"

The tears fell freely, and the woman put her face in her hands and sobbed. Another woman held her while she cried.

"Elsie was there for me too." The speaker, his blue eyes filled with tears, was a man wearing a lab coat with the name Dr. Robert Alms, Oncology Department, embroidered over his heart. "When I was an intern, she would make suggestions to me about patient care. Thank God I listened to her. She kept me from making some pretty fundamental mistakes. She was always looking out for the new interns. She taught me so much." Dr. Alms was crying openly, and several nurses moved to his side.

Another person took up where he had left off and told another story. The stories continued along with the tears, and the warm, wonderful person who was Elsie came alive once more in that room.

# Chapter Nine

"You're going to be late for morning report!" Nick walked by me, brandishing his large cappuccino. I was still in the coffee line, silently hating the people ordering the complicated lattes and cappuccinos. If they just ordered coffee, there wouldn't be this line. There were five people ahead of me, and the meeting was starting in five minutes. Did I have time to get coffee? I felt like a squirrel trying to cross the road.

"You're late," Ted said. The group stared at me as I made my way to the only open chair around the table.

"I'm sorry."

"Okay, let's see." Ted was looking at the chaplain sheets. "Julie, I see you did a baptism yesterday. How did that go?"

Judy, Beth, and Frank were quiet and thoughtful as I related the story of the baptism. Nick was visibly disturbed, and his audible sighs were strong enough to move the foam on top of his cappuccino.

"Nick, is there something wrong?" asked Ted.

"Yeah, she baptized a dead baby!" He looked around the room. "Doesn't anyone have a problem with that?"

"You baptized a suicidal man, remember? Someone unable to make a decision about anything much less his spiritual life!" Beth glared at Nick. "Chaplains are not supposed to impose their beliefs on the patients. Remember?"

"You don't even believe in baptism. You're Unitarian."

Beth rolled her eyes. "I'm not going down that road again, Nick."

"Julie, why don't you tell us how you feel about it?" Ted asked.

"Awful. I felt awful about it. The nurse looked traumatized, and the poor young mother was devastated. I was trying to figure out the best thing to do. My mind was racing with all the stuff I had learned as a child about unbaptized babies not going to heaven and that dead people could not be baptized. I didn't know what to do, so I prayed."

"Aha, and what happened?" Ted sat back in his chair.

"I heard a distinct voice in my head say 'Baptize the baby.'"

"So you did."

"Yes, I did. I did it for the mother and the nurses. I felt like the three of us were acknowledging this brief life, and baptism was the best way to do that."

"So, you think God told you to baptize the baby?" Nick had jumped up out of his seat and was leaning over the table.

"I would have done it," said Frank, the Roman Catholic priest, who rarely participated in these kinds of discussions. He was sixty-five and was very secure in his ideas about pastoral care. He was in the process of leaving his parish and becoming a hospital chaplain, so he had decided to take a unit of Clinical Pastoral Education.

"I know your church doesn't believe in baptizing the dead. So why on earth baptize the dead?" Nick turned to stare at Frank.

"For the living, Nick. For the living."

"Well, every time we get together we hear about God talking to Julie in these short, pithy sentences. I don't really believe that God is telling you this stuff, Julie. You just think this stuff up and do whatever you want."

"All I know is that whatever the short, pithy sentences tell me to do seems to work well, so I'm sticking with the praying." I took a sip of my coffee.

"Oh yeah, and what would you like God to tell you now?" Nick's tone dripped sarcasm.

"Actually, I would love to know if the prayer service I did yesterday for the woman who was killed in the drive-by shooting was okay. I've never done anything like it before, and I would love to get some feedback."

"Wow, what a selfish request." Nick threw his hands in the air. "So, go ahead and ask God."

"Fine. God, please let me know if I did a good job at the prayer service, Amen."

Ted sighed. "All right, enough, time to go back up to the units."

The group got up and started to file out of the tiny conference room. As we stepped out into the hallway, a large group of people was just getting on the set of elevators next to the conference room. I recognized one of the women. She had told the first story at the prayer service. I smiled at her. She put her hand in between the elevator doors just as they started to close and forced them open so she could step out.

"You're the one!" she said.

The group of chaplains stopped to listen.

"You're the one who did the prayer service yesterday."

I nodded.

"I just want to tell you that the service was wonderful, and we really appreciated what you did for us."

I glanced at Nick. His mouth hung open, his eyes were wide, and as he slowly turned to look at me, I winked at him.

"Thank you, Dolores," I said reading her name tag. "You are an answer to a prayer."

## Chapter Ten

I could hear his screams the second the elevator door opened. It was the bone-chilling, ear-piercing sound of an animal trying to escape a trap. The intensity made me run down the dimly lit hallway. I wondered why I had been called. The man was obviously in agony. He needed more than a chaplain.

All the lights were on in the unit, and patients were hovering around the doors to their rooms, trying to get a look. The largest group of hospital staff was gathered around the entrance to one of the rooms. Had there been an accident? I had never seen more than one sleepy intern and a few nurses working in the hospital at 3:00 a.m.

"Doctor, there's the chaplain." One of the nurses had spotted me. All I saw was her finger pointing at me. Her lips were moving, but I couldn't hear any sound. The screaming was that loud. The man was thrashing around in the bed. He was pulling at the restraints digging into his wrists and ankles. His face was red, and I could clearly see the veins in his neck.

"What is going on?" I yelled at the doctor.

He threw up his hands. "He's had enough medication to put down an elephant, but he won't stop screaming. We can't give him anything else or we'll kill him." He looked at me. "We were hoping that you could do something." They were all looking at me.

"Get this crowd out of his room." My first thought was this man does not need an audience. He continued to scream and thrash. I watched him. His eyes were closed, and his face was scrunched up with pain. I know this man, I thought. He was the patient whose wife had motioned to me as I was passing by his room earlier in the day.

"Are you the chaplain?"

"Yes," I said. "What gave it away?"

She laughed. I was wearing a cross and carrying a Bible.

"I wanted you to meet my husband," she said. "He needs prayers." Her husband had been diagnosed with Alzheimer's three years ago. She had taken care of him until it became obvious that he was getting too hard to handle. At first, he had followed her around placidly, obeying all of her requests. But as his memory dimmed, and as he became more and more confused, he began to get agitated. He wouldn't go where she told him to go. He didn't want to sit or lie down. He just wanted to walk. She was constantly taking him to the table or to an easy chair. He would sit for a minute and then get right up and want to go somewhere else. It was exhausting.

Their children persuaded her to put her husband in a home. He needed a safe place, and they thought he might hurt their mother. He could escape from the house and go wandering. He needed nursing care. Just tracking his medicine was time consuming. Reluctantly, she gave in and found him a place close by their house. For the last two years, she had faithfully spent every day with the man who had been her husband for over fifty years. She fed him his meals, read him the newspaper, and walked with him. Up and down the hallway they walked. The companionship from these walks was all that she felt she had left of him.

He had stopped talking soon after he had entered the home. She missed the sound of his voice, but in some ways it was a relief. She didn't have to answer his questions that didn't make sense or feel the need to try to reorient him. His mind had become disconnected. She looked into his eyes, and he looked back without any recognition. It was like looking at a zombie. He was the walking dead.

The routine of feeding him, reading to him, and walking with him went on for several months. Then the screaming started. At first it was just groans. It began at night when he was put to bed. The staff increased his sleeping pills. Then there was the weight loss. In a few short weeks, he looked like a scarecrow. His clothes hung loosely on his body. His pants stayed on with the help of a belt borrowed from a smaller patient. He walked through the hallways looking like someone who had just escaped from a concentration camp.

One of his adult children, who lived on the other side of the country, showed up at the home. He was shocked and insisted that the medical staff figure out what was wrong with his father. After many tests and much screaming, they found out he had pancreatic cancer. Now it was just a matter of time before his body joined his mind.

"If only you had known him," his wife said to me as she stroked his hand. He was sitting in a Geri chair. I hated to see adults locked in a chair by a table that fit over the arms like a high chair. I knew the table was there to keep the patient safe. The chair made it impossible for the occupant to get up. Still, it looked degrading.

His wife continued, "He was the chief financial officer at one of the local companies. All his employees loved him and ..." She hesitated. Her face tightened. "He was a good man. He went to church every Sunday, and he sang in the choir." She looked at me. "He was a good man," she repeated.

"Yes," I said. She continued to tell me stories of all the wonderful things her husband had done, and how everyone had loved him. I watched him stare vacantly ahead. His wife reached out and wiped the drool off his chin.

Now this same man was screaming and thrashing. It was the most alive I had seen him. I stood there feeling helpless. "Good Lord, let me help this man," I prayed. I was at a total loss. His screams were so loud.

All of a sudden, a thought came into my head. Music soothes the wild beast. I should sing something, but I couldn't think of anything to sing. The screams were intensifying. In desperation, I began to sing "Amazing Grace." His head turned toward the sound. He continued to scream. I was singing and at the same time thinking, I only know one verse. What will I do when the verse ends? No other thoughts came, so I stopped singing. He stopped screaming. For a brief moment there was silence. Total silence. And then, in a clear baritone voice, he began to sing. He sang the second verse, the third verse, and all the way through to the sixth verse. All activity on the unit ceased. The sound of his voice floated through the hallway and carried all of us to a place where cancer and Alzheimer's did not exist.

When he finished singing, he closed his eyes and appeared to go to sleep. The staff and I were stunned. For a few minutes, nobody moved. Then very quietly the staff who had had gathered outside during his singing went back to work. I stood there dumbfounded. I could still hear his singing in my head. I sat next to his bed, grabbed a pen and some scrap paper, and wrote his wife a note. "I heard your husband sing, and it was amazing!"

The next day he left the hospital. A few months later, his wife wrote to tell me that he had died and that part of her was relieved and part of her was terribly sad, but all of her was glad that he had woken up one last time to sing.

As I wandered through the halls of the hospital the next few days, I kept hearing his voice. It had moved from my head into my heart. The melody kept playing over and over along with the words "How precious did that grace appear, the hour I first believed." What was grace? I wondered. Of course, I had studied grace in seminary, and I had come to know it as the love and forgiveness freely given to us by God. Now, I knew grace could come unbidden through the most unexpected messengers and manifest itself in the midst of the most difficult situations, and it was somehow related to prayer. My walks through the halls were full of feelings of thanksgiving. I couldn't stop thinking about it.

## *Chapter Eleven*

There was something familiar about the shrill voice screaming about proper patient care.

"I told you I want her to get physical therapy." The voice was high, like she had just swallowed some helium.

"Your mother isn't ready for physical therapy." This voice was calm and barely audible.

I turned the corner, and the two voices became people. One was a woman dressed in jean shorts and a T-shirt that said "Walker Family Reunion." The other woman I recognized as the social worker assigned to the floor. There was something about the woman in the T-shirt. I knew I had seen her before.

The social worker put her hand on the woman's arm. "Alice, please try to understand. Your mother is too weak for therapy."

Alice! This was the daughter whose mother had been dying in intensive care. I had met her on my on-call night. In that same moment, Alice recognized me.

"Oh, there's the chaplain. Remember me? My mother is so much better now! Have you come to pray with her again?" She ran over and threw her arms around me.

"Where is your mother?" I asked.

"Over there," Alice said as she pointed to a room.

A forest of IV trees surrounded her mother's bed, bags hanging like ripe fruit just before harvest—eleven of them. A monitor tracked heart rate, blood pressure, oxygen levels, and some other statistics.

"They said she wouldn't live." Alice took her mother's hand. "Look at her. She's doing great. Mom! Mom!" Her mother didn't budge.

"She has a lot of IV bags," I offered, hoping that I might find out why Alice seemed so optimistic about her mother's progress.

"She needs a lot of medicine." Alice stared at one of the bags. "She had thirteen bags in ICU."

"Really? So, what happened to your mother?"

"She got sick and came to the hospital. I've been working real hard to get her back home again. I know I can take care of her." Alice reached up and turned off a beeping IV machine. She smiled at me. "See, I watch the nurses." She grabbed my hand.

"You need to pray for her." Her nails were digging into my skin. "God will help her, I know it. She's a good woman."

A herd of white coats entered the room and circled the bed. Alice released my hand and went to the head of the bed. "I'm her daughter." The young doctors said nothing.

Another white coat entered the room. The man's hair matched his coat. He slowly made his way over to Alice, stopping occasionally to look at one of the IV poles. The wrinkles in his tanned face deepened when he smiled gently at Alice.

"She's still here, Doctor," Alice said.

"Yes, she is." The doctor picked up the mother's hand and examined the IV line sticking out of her wrist.

"It's a miracle, isn't it?"

"Yes, Alice." The doctor placed the mother's hand back on the bed and motioned to the circle of white coats, and they all followed him out.

After a short prayer with Alice, I went to the nurse's station and got her mother's chart. Alice's mother had cancer in almost every organ of her body. She'd been here for a week. Her daughter had insisted on life support and aggressive chemo treatments. The chemo had been stopped, but she remained on life support. The social worker saw me looking at the chart.

"And she wants her to have physical therapy." She shook her head. "She doesn't want to let her mother go."

That seemed like an understatement. I said a prayer for Alice. Please, God, help her to let go, I prayed as I walked into another room on the unit.

The man in this room was so large that his body spilled over the sides of the bed. When he saw me, his face lit up and his rosy-red lips formed a huge toothy smile in the middle of his frothy white beard. In contrast to Alice's mother with her forest of IV poles, this man had nothing around him. The room was bare, not even a chair.

"Hi, I'm the chaplain." I stood awkwardly next to his bed.

"I'm Ed. Just so you know, God's gonna take care of me."

"Well, that's good," I replied.

"Yeah, I have some medical condition, but I don't believe in doctors or hospitals." He crossed his arms over his massive chest. The hospital gown strained at the seams.

"So, why are you here?"

"My son said I had to come, but he can't make me get treatment. They tell me I need a blood transfusion, but I'm not going to get it." He was watching me, waiting for my reaction.

"Why not?" I was beginning to think I should have looked at his chart before I came in here.

His face had gotten serious, and he looked right at me.

"Because God is the healer and the only healer. He is going to cure me and no one else. I'm a Jehovah's Witness. We believe that taking blood into our bodies through mouth or veins violates God's law."

"So what if you have to have the blood or you will die?" I struggled to keep my voice even and my face expressionless.

"Well, then I guess God wants me to die." He settled back into the bed and smiled.

"Dad?" A younger-looking version of the man in the bed entered the room. His beard was brown, but the eyes and the smile were the same.

"Son, this is the chaplain."

"I'm not a Jehovah's Witness," I said quickly.

"Good. Then maybe you can help convince my dad that he needs to let go of all that crazy stuff so we can save his life."

"Uh, I'm not supposed to push my beliefs onto anyone," I said nervously.

"Then what are you supposed to do?" The son edged closer to me and looked down on me. He was probably twelve inches taller.

"Help people clarify their own beliefs and try to be a source of spiritual comfort." I stood my ground.

The son stared at me for a moment. "Oh, so then you can be one of the people who watches him die." He turned and left the room.

# Chapter Twelve

The chapel was empty. I fell into one of the only comfortable chairs and closed my eyes. I could almost always count on the chapel as a place I could hide out and rest. If I was caught, I could always say I was praying. I kept seeing Ed's smile in my head, but his son's question hung in my mind. What was I supposed to be doing? Sometimes it just seemed like I was going from room to room watching crazy situations play out in front of me like some macabre version of reality television. My hands were tied as a chaplain. There was nothing I could "do" and practically nothing I could say. I couldn't imagine that I was being helpful.

The chapel door opened. Ted, my supervisor, strolled in and sat down in the chair across from me.

"What's going on?" he asked.

"I'm useless. I just listen to people."

"And what would you like to be doing?"

"Helping them!" I was frustrated. "Nancy Walker is dying of cancer, she's hooked up to eleven IV bags, and her daughter wants her to have physical therapy. There's a man in the room next door who needs a blood transfusion and won't get it because his religion doesn't believe in any medical procedures."

Ted closed his eyes.

"What are you doing?"

"Praying."

I sighed. Nick was right. I didn't really believe in the pithy little voice I kept hearing in my head. Perhaps these "answers" were really coming from me. Now I was irritated. I just wanted some answers. My whole career in corporate America had been about fixing problems and providing solutions.

Ted's wrinkles had smoothed out. Was he sleeping? I closed my eyes and sat quietly.

It was there. The voice was there. "Help Alice let go," it said.

"What about Ed?" Nothing. "Come on, God, what about Ed? God, are you there?" Nothing.

"Ted?"

He opened his eyes. "Yes?"

"The voice was there."

He leaned forward in his chair. "What did it say?"

"Help Alice let go of her mother, Nancy."

"That makes sense."

"But there was nothing about the blood transfusion, so I'm not sure what to do with him."

"Maybe there is nothing to do with him."

"You mean just watch him die?"

"Sounds like he's okay with it."

"It's like a form of suicide!"

"We can't give treatment to someone who doesn't want it. Just keep listening, Julie. Sometimes it just takes time to see where things are going." Ted stood up and stretched. "I've got an appointment."

I looked at the twenty-third Psalm written on the chapel wall. I went back to the floor.

*Chapter Thirteen*

The cafeteria was nearly deserted. There were two people eating a late lunch, one scanning the paper and the other reading a paperback novel. The trash cans were overflowing with the remains of a crowded lunch hour. Trays of half-eaten food were scattered among the tables. It was a familiar sight. Medical staff would be in the middle of a meal and then their pager would go off. They would stand up in unison like a choir getting up to sing a hymn, leave their food behind, and rush out the door.

Where was Al? I wondered. He was usually here at three in the afternoon. My watch said just three, and as I turned to leave, I saw Al at the cash register buying his Dove Bar. He caught sight of me, waved, gave me the "just a minute sign" and disappeared back into the kitchen area. I sat down at one of the cleaner tables.

"Hey, Julie." He sat down across from me and slid a Dove Bar across the table. I stared at it. Milk chocolate with vanilla ice cream. Three hundred and thirty delicious, mouth-watering calories.

"Go ahead, eat it. It's good for the soul," Al said, biting into his and licking his lips. "Besides, aren't you on call today? You never know when you'll get a chance to eat."

Al was right. I had gotten the pager from Judy at report. So far, it hadn't made a sound, but I had plenty of days where I never made it into the cafeteria.

I picked up the bar and pulled off the wrapping.

"So, what brings you here today?" Al smiled. He was a permanent Roman Catholic chaplain at the hospital. The supervisors in the chaplains' office said he was the priest who had the fastest thumb in the west. This meant that Al would get the census of all the Roman Catholic patients and go anoint them with oil. He would record this in the "anointing book" in the hope that he would not be called out of his nice comfortable bed in the middle of the night to give "last rites." No matter how many times he would reassure the family that their loved one was good to go, they would page him at all hours of the day or night for last rites. Al was as close as you could get to being an expert in death and dying. He had been at the hospital for twenty years, and there were only a few constants in Al's life: rarely sleeping through the night, death, and for the last twenty years, his three o'clock Dove Bar. This Dove Bar routine, he said, was the only way he could deal with the suffering.

"I got two people in God's waiting room," I said. This expression came from Al. It was the one he used to calm anxious family members.

"Do they need anointing?"

"No. One needs to die, but her daughter is keeping her going by telling her she's going to get over a cancer that's spread through every organ in her body. The other one could live a pretty good and healthy life, but he's going to die because he's a Jehovah's Witness and they don't allow transfusions." I was feeling better. The ice cream was having the desired affect. The milk chocolate shell combined with the creamy vanilla flavor was a melted mass of exquisite sweetness in my mouth.

"Hmmm." Al was in the throes of his daily afternoon treat. We sat and ate. I had never felt so comforted. The old priest had a drip of chocolate on his chin. He smiled at me as he wiped it away. Then he reached into his pocket, pulled out his oil, and anointed me just as my pager went off.

There was a motorcycle helmet on the chair outside the trauma area. I could see my face in the shiny black finish. I reached up to feel my cheek because I thought I had gotten cut somehow. My fingers touched smooth skin. It was the helmet. There was a long and jagged crack in the helmet.

"Where's the blood?" a voice demanded.

"I need some help here." Another voice.

"Pressure!" Multiple voices were sounding more desperate.

I stayed in the corner and prayed. I didn't know what to pray for, so I kept praying, "Oh God, Oh God, Oh God," over and over. The man on the table looked incredibly young. His partially grown beard had spots of skin showing through, and where his moustache should have been, there were only a few stray hairs.

A nurse pulled me aside. "Here, take his wallet and see if you can find a next of kin. I've paged a social worker, but I haven't seen one yet." She rushed off.

The thin, worn, black wallet displayed a Colorado's driver's license and a twenty-dollar bill. I looked at the name, Jim DeAngelo. The license said he was sixty.

The unit secretary poked her head around the curtain and came over. "Can he have visitors?" she asked. As the words came out of her mouth, she shook her head and retreated. I got up to see who the visitors were.

A group of five teenage boys stood huddled together in the corner of the waiting room. Three were talking on their cell phones. One of the boys saw me coming.

"Is Jimmy alright?" His face was devoid of color. He clutched a leather jacket with such force the veins of his hands stood out.

"They're doing the best they can," I said. "I need some information. Do you know his next of kin?"

"Oh God, Oh God." He was hyperventilating. "He's dead, isn't he? Oh God, Oh, God."

"No, but I need his next of kin.

He was silent.

"Look, I know the license isn't his, but I need to know his next of kin." I handed him a piece of paper, and he wrote out a name and address just in time for me to hand it to the social worker.

While she called the parents, I went back into the trauma area. There was blood everywhere. The boy's face was puffed, swollen, and barely recognizable from even a few minutes ago. I continued to pray for everyone: the doctors, the parents who were right now getting the call that every parent dreads, the kids in the waiting room, and most of all, the boy on the table who was clinging to life. I had never before felt more helpless, and I wasn't alone. The medical staff was focused, but I could see in everyone's eyes that they knew they were fighting a losing battle. But they didn't give up. They continued until it was apparent that there was nothing left to do. Blood oozed out faster than it could drip in, and all of it was too much, even for the boy's strong, young heart.

"Time of death, five o'clock."

His eyelids were cool to my touch. I gently closed them, and we stood there while I prayed. I prayed again for all of us. How difficult it was for the staff to watch a young life literally drain away.

"His parents are here." It was the unit secretary. She took in the scene and then quickly turned away. "I'll bring them to the conference room."

"You better get him ready," one of the doctors said, "They'll probably want to see him."

I was back in the small windowless conference room, but this time it was a man and woman close to my age who were sitting on the love seat, holding each other's hand. They looked up hopefully when I walked into the room followed by three doctors. One doctor sat in the chair, and the other two stood next to him. I closed the door. The woman glanced at my name badge and started to cry softly.

"We did everything we could," said the doctor in the chair. At this, the man started to breath hard. He looked panicked.

One of the other doctors spoke. "He had multiple fractures, his arms, his legs—"

"He's dead?" The father stood, pulling his wife up with him. "He cannot be dead. He can't die. I told him he would never die. Not like his uncle, not like his uncle." The mother, who had collapsed back onto the love seat, had tears streaming down her face. The father started to pace in the tiny room. Two steps in one direction, turn, two more steps, turn.

The doctor stood up and joined the others. "Do you have any questions?" The emergency room doctor, the orthopedic surgeon, and the neurosurgeon were all backing out of the room.

The father's pain had overflowed. The room could not contain the intensity of the emotion. Please, God, tell me what to do, I prayed silently.

"Who is Jim DeAngelo?" The sound of my own voice startled me.

The father stopped pacing and sat back down on the couch.

"Jim was his uncle." His voice was hoarse. "He was my older brother, and Jimmy was named after him." The father put his hands over his face. "Jim died in Vietnam. I named my son after him." He looked up at me. "He was the same age as Jimmy when he died in Vietnam."

A nurse came to the door and motioned me outside. "They can come and see his body, but they can't stay long, and they have to come now."

"Why?"

"Because, he's full of blood, and it's leaking out of every pore. We have his body wrapped in blankets but it will start seeping out."

It couldn't get any worse.

We took the elevator down one floor and followed the nurse to a secluded area near the surgical recovery unit. As soon as I pulled the curtain back, the mother went to the bed and started to cry. The father hung back. I put my arm around his mother and held her as she cried. The nurse escorted the father in, and as soon as he got to the side of the bed he collapsed and fainted. His wife and I knelt next to him while the nurse ran for help. He opened his eyes and looked at me. "I told him he couldn't die. Why has God done this to us? Why did God take him too?" He was grabbing my shirt and pulling me down right to his face. "Answer me!" He let go and closed his eyes.

The waiting room was now full of teenagers. The cell phones had worked their magic, and there were over twenty young people milling around. I herded them all into the now-vacant trauma unit still caked with blood and littered with scraps of packaging. As they entered, some fell silent and some started to cry.

I looked at the boy still clutching the leather coat. "What happened?"

"We were all riding on the highway around the city." He stopped and started to cry. "Jimmy doesn't have a motorcycle license, but he wanted to go." He took a deep breath. "We were doing eighty around the curve, and he crashed into the concrete wall."

Another boy came forward. "Jimmy always said he was immortal. He said nothing could happen to him if he had his uncle's license. He said his uncle was watching over him."

Stupid, stupid boys, I thought. I felt myself grow angry at the thought process that had led to the risky behavior. It was frightening. I struggled not to think about my own sons. But the energy from the anger transformed itself into a question. What could I do for the living?

"No one is immortal." I pointed to the blood on the floor and then looked back at the original five boys. "That could have easily have been any one of you. You were probably going even faster. You all think you're immortal. You're not." I practically spit the words out.

One of the other boys said, "What can we do? He's gone now, forever."

"You can help his parents get through this," I said. "They're really going to need your help."

I spent another two hours talking with the boys and their friends. They wanted to know why he had died. I had to convince them it was because Jimmy was going eighty around a curve designed for half that speed. This has nothing to do with his uncle, I insisted as they continued to argue with me. No one gets a free pass from bad choices. While we talked, a staff person cleaned up the mess, washed down the floor, picked up the countless scraps of paper, and rearranged the supplies in order to be ready for the next crisis. He slowly and meticulously put things back in order. It took a long time. He was still at it when I left.

# Chapter Fourteen

I was back in Ted's office watching him crunch on a salad like a middle-aged cow grazing in a meadow of thick grass. I felt like the bee trying to get the cow's attention. I had been buzzing with the descriptions of all the people I had seen and all their tragedies.

"Am I boring you?" I asked.

"No, you're not boring me. I'm just waiting for you to get to what's really on your mind."

"Isn't it enough that some teenager killed himself on a motorcycle and I had to bring the parents in to see his body? What else could possibly be on my mind?"

He sat there munching in silence, his mouth full of lettuce.

"How could he do that to his family? He was going eighty miles an hour around a curve. He must have wanted to die."

Ted leaned back in his chair, balancing on the two back legs, and swallowed. "What did his friends say?"

"His friends said they were just out joyriding."

"So how does that become a suicide?" Ted crossed his arms behind his head. I sat there glaring, angry with him for asking me these ridiculous questions, angry with the kid for dying, and angry with a God who didn't protect teenage boys.

"Don't they have to have some judgment before they get a motorcycle license? Isn't there some safety program they have to take? Who goes out and joyrides at eighty miles per hour?" I clenched the sides of my chair like I was hanging on for dear life. I did not want to believe that this could happen.

"This is what some teenage boys do," Ted said calmly as he reached for his salad.

"Not my teenage boys!" I cried in my don't-you-dare-do-it mother's voice.

"Aha! So that's what this is about. Your boys." Ted put the rest of his salad in the garbage. "You're afraid."

"Of course I'm afraid." My voice sounded high-pitched and squeaky. And then quietly I said, "I don't want to be the parent in the emergency room."

"You aren't the parent in the emergency room."

"But I could be the parent in the emergency room." I was close to crying now. There was a lump in my throat and tightness in my chest as I pictured myself in the room, identifying the body of one of my boys.

"Julie, it's not you. You can't put yourself in every one of these situations. It's important that you keep yourself separated or you won't be able to help anyone. People need a non-anxious presence. Someone they can hold onto, someone who is grounded, someone who is not falling apart."

"You didn't have to listen to the father screaming why at the top of his lungs. 'Why did God let my son die?'"

This perked his interest. "What did you say?" Ted asked.

"Nothing, what could I say?" I countered. "I know God didn't force that child to ride his motorcycle at an unsafe speed. But where was God in all of that?"

I stared out the window at a bright sunny day. People were eating their lunches out on the lawn, and everything seemed normal. How deceiving, I thought. Life was anything but bright, sunny, and normal. Ted's phone rang. My time with him was over, so he reached for it. Before he picked it up, he looked at me and said, "God was with the son, the father, the mother, the nurse, and you.

# Chapter Fifteen

"Julie, you're needed up in pediatrics intensive care."

I was in no mood for whatever awaited me in the peds ICU. Tension made my whole body ache.

It was 5:00 p.m. A crowd of people moaning and crying huddled outside one of the rooms. My hopes of leaving the hospital by six seemed to fade fast. God help me, I mouthed silently as I moved toward the room.

A nurse bent over the small body lying on the bed. She jerked her head toward me when the door opened. "Who are you?" she snapped.

"I'm the chaplain." The body in the bed was a little girl. Her dark black hair was braided with pink ribbons and beads. The breathing tube was taped on her face with white adhesive tape. It looked so out of place on her soft dark skin.

"Sorry." There was blood on the front of the nurse's shirt. Little yellow ducks covered with drops of bright red blood. The nurse quickly wiped her eyes. "This is a tough one. We don't think she's going to make it."

"What happened?" I asked. I saw the little girl's pink shirt, shorts, and sneakers on the chair. At first, I thought they were dirty, but then I realized the brown was dried bloodstains.

"There was a car accident, a mom and her four daughters. The EMTs don't think this little one was wearing a seat belt. Her neck was broken." The nurse sucked in her breath and paused for a moment. "She's paralyzed from the neck down. They don't know the extent of all her injuries, but the doctors don't seem very hopeful."

I stared at the little face on the pillow.

"Her mom is in the trauma unit, and her three sisters are in the pediatric ward."

"Has anyone called the father?"

"They're getting him from prison."

"Prison?" All of this felt like a fire hose of tragedy. I couldn't begin to conceive what this mother was up against.

"Yes, in cases like this, they sometimes let relatives come and say good-bye. He's on his way with two guards. We thought you could help him say good-bye." The nurse smoothed the sheets and gently stroked the little girl's head. "She just turned five. The people in the hallway said she was so excited about going to kindergarten next year."

"Who are all the people in the hallway?" I asked. I couldn't take my eyes off the little girl's face.

"They're her church family. Apparently, the church rallied around the mother when her husband went to prison. It's like the entire church is here. They just seem to love this little girl. They want to come in here and pray, but we thought it would be better if we called one of our chaplains to help. They've been waiting for you. You can bring them in a few at a time." The nurse patted the little girl's head and left the room.

I stood, totally numb, afraid to move in case my feelings came pouring out. Not wearing a seat belt? Is that what the nurse had said? It was not my place to pass judgment, but I wanted someone to blame. The cover that was holding my feelings inside was starting to quiver. I needed to turn down the heat and stop the boiling, so I prayed, "Please, God, help me." There was a quiet knock on the door, and two women and a man from the hallway stepped inside.

"We're her church family," one woman said and then burst into tears. "Oh, my baby, my baby, what happened to you?" She laid her body across the bed on top of the little girl's chest and began to cry with loud, wrenching sobs punctuated by high-pitched cries. "My little girl, my little girl." The second woman began crying, and in a loud voice prayed for Jesus to come and take her baby home. The man began to pray in a very loud and low voice asking Jesus for help. I just stood there watching and letting their feelings merge with mine, and then I started crying too.

"What's going on here?" The nurse with the yellow baby-duck shirt almost ran into the room. She glared at me and then turned to the two women and the man and said, "You must calm down. You cannot be shouting and carrying on like this! This is an intensive care unit. You are disturbing the other patients." She turned to me. "This is why you were paged. Good heavens, do your job and help these people! There are more of them in the hall."

The nurse's tone was like being doused with icy-cold water. I took a deep breath and sprang into action.

"Let's go, you three. Out into the hall." I grabbed the woman lying prostrate on the little girl and pulled her off the bed. The others followed me.

"Excuse me," I said loudly. "Would Tanya's family follow me?" No one was listening. I went around to each little group. "Are you here for Tanya? Please go to the family waiting room." It was like herding cats. I'd get a few people to start in the direction of the waiting room and then another group would distract them.

In the midst of this, I was suddenly aware of Ted leaning up against the wall in the hallway. He motioned to me. "How's it going?"

"Not good."

"Have you heard of the Jesus Prayer?" He was holding out a little black rope with knots about every quarter inch. It looked like a bracelet with a small black tassel.

"No." Leave it to Ted; in the middle of some of the worst chaos, he's trying to teach me a prayer? What I really needed was a way to organize this group of crazed people.

"It's easy. Lord Jesus Christ, have mercy on me. Just say it over and over."

"Really?" Well, that should solve all my problems, I thought. I closed my eyes. "Lord Jesus Christ, have mercy on me," I whispered softly. Ted was gone, and I was standing there in the crowded hallway holding the black prayer rope. A thought came to me that I was to assert my authority and get this crowd under control.

"Everyone! You will be asked to leave if you do not go immediately to the family waiting room. Security will be called." The crowd got quiet. "The family waiting room is just down the hall to the left." I pointed in the direction of the room, and the crowd slowly obliged.

I herded the stragglers into the waiting room, closed the door, climbed up on a chair, and addressed the group. "Is the pastor here from Tanya's church?"

An older man dressed in an olive-green suit came forward.

"Pastor, can you organize the group here to pray for Tanya? She needs prayers."

"What's wrong with our baby?" A voice from the crowd asked. The woman who had covered Tanya's bed answered, "They think she's paralyzed from the neck down, and she may not make it." She started crying loudly.

"Quiet! You cannot cry and carry on here. It will not help Tanya. She needs your prayers and help, not your hysteria. Think of her. Please, pastor, get this group to start praying."

"When can we see her?" another voice asked.

"I'll come and get you a few at a time." I got off the chair when I heard a commotion in the hallway. I heard the chains before I saw them. The father shuffled down the hall in his shackles, his eyes darting left and right searching for his little girl, a guard at each elbow. He would have looked like a child himself if he hadn't been so tall—well over six feet. He had a baby face and wide, oval, deep-set eyes. His hands were clasped in front of him in a position of prayer. I grasped the little black prayer rope and in my head kept repeating, "Lord Jesus Christ, have mercy on me, Lord Jesus Christ, have mercy on me ..."

"Tanya's dad?" I asked as I walked up to the prisoner and put my hands over his hands.

"Is she still alive?" His red-rimmed eyes searched me as if I was hiding the answer in my face.

"Yes, she's resting. Her injuries are severe, but she is still alive. I can take you to her."

The men followed me to Tanya's room. When the father saw his little girl, his legs buckled, and he crashed to the floor. Both guards pulled him up and dragged him over to the bed. The father's eyes were squeezed shut, and he was shaking his head back and forth saying, "No, no, no, no ..."

I touched his hands again and said, "Let's pray. I held hands with the father and one of the guards, and the four of us bowed our heads.

Later, I talked with one of the guards in the hallway. He was watching the father through the window of a small conference room, where he was talking with his wife. She was in a wheel chair. They were both crying and holding each other.

"I have a five-year-old." The guard rubbed his eyes. "Paralyzed, I can't imagine."

"Me neither. Thank God it's not our kids," I said, willing myself to be the non-anxious presence.

"Yeah." The guard straightened himself and continued his watch.

I went back into the little girl's room. She appeared to be sleeping peacefully, but I knew by now it was probably the drugs dripping into her arm. I picked up her hand. Her tiny fingernails had splotches of pink nail polish. Just a few days ago, she had been painting her nails, and now she was here fighting for her life. I stayed for a while holding her hand and praying the Jesus Prayer, my new anchor. It steadied me, and I hoped it was helping Tanya. She lay like a frozen snow angel. I got up, kissed her forehead, and went home.

# Chapter Sixteen

A few days later, Ted caught me at the coffee shop. He listened intently as I described the scene outside and inside Tanya's room. "Is the prayer helping?" he asked, sipping his tea.

"I guess so." I shrugged. Helping what, I wondered? Was it keeping me from totally losing it, or was it helping the poor paralyzed five-year-old? Clutching the prayer rope did seem to help me feel better about taking charge and introducing crowd control when I needed to.

"Have you heard anything about Tanya?" I asked.

"Actually, I checked on her this morning." Ted took out his teabag, squeezed out the excess tea, and threw it in the garbage. "She's going to live, but she is paralyzed from the neck down."

My throat tightened. "That's what the nurse said."

"Yup, I heard she's awake. Maybe you should go visit her before you go up to your floor." He had finished putting cream and sugar in his cup and was already heading down the hall.

I started my daily trek up the steps. I hesitated when I got to the fourth floor and wondered if I should see her or not.

The door to Tanya's room was open, and there was a nurse feeding her a Popsicle.

"Oh good," the nurse said. "Can you take over?" She handed me the Popsicle.

Tanya's doelike eyes followed the Popsicle. "Can I have some more?"

"Sure, sweetheart." I pulled a chair close to the bed and put the Popsicle up to her mouth. Her lips were cherry red, the same color as the Popsicle. She continued licking.

"How do you feel?" I asked.

She stopped licking and turned her head toward me. "Okay, I guess." She took another lick. "I can't walk, and I can't use my arms. I'm like that doll." Her head nodded at a rag doll on the bed.

The tears flooded my eyes, and I tried to wink them back, but it was too late. She had stopped eating and was staring at me. My hand reached into my pocket and clutched at the black prayer rope. "Lord Jesus Christ, have mercy on me," I said under my breath. How awful, I thought, crying in front of a severely injured child.

"Don't be sad." She said. "Lots of people are sad, but I'm not. My family loves me, and I have lots and lots of family." She smiled. Drips of red juice ran down her face. "The doctor said that people will take care of me just like I took care of my doll." She looked at me, her eyes narrowing. "And I took very good care of my doll." She finished the Popsicle. I got up to leave. "Can you put Julie next to me in the bed under the covers?"

"Julie? Her name is Julie?" I was dumbfounded.

"Yep, she needs lots of love and cuddles just like me." Tanya laughed at my surprised expression. "I keep her happy!"

"I bet you do." I carefully placed the doll under the covers next to Tanya. "God bless you, Tanya."

"God bless you too; uh, what's your name?"

"Julie."

Her eyes grew wide. "Just like my doll?"

"Just like your doll."

"Well, I will take care of you too!" She giggled happily.

"Thank you," I said as I left the room, with a picture of the little girl and the rag doll propped up in bed together stuck in my head. Tanya had taken care of me. I couldn't help but think she had no idea about what her new life would be like, and maybe for her, this was a game. I certainly hadn't expected her to be happy. Imagine her telling me in that cute little voice that she would take care of me. I suddenly realized that I had heard many patients reassuring loved ones about their condition, particularly those who were dying. They always seemed to be the ones comforting the healthy people. Right before I had started CPE, I went to see a friend of mine who had been diagnosed with terminal brain cancer. I stood in her hospital room and wailed, "Oh Donna, I wish there was something I could do." Donna, with her baldhead sticking up out of her hospital gown, looked me squarely in the eye, smiled, and said, "You can come give me a hug; that's what you can do." And now, a five-year-old quadriplegic girl had just ministered to me. She had been confident that she could take care of me, and she had. Something was coming into my awareness about how to be present. I needed to let go of any kind of judgment or expectations that I might have for the patients I encountered. My role was to be a reminder of God's love for them. That meant accepting their condition and their own reaction to it. I began to focus on just being with people, listening, and repeating back their observations so they could hear their own thoughts. Sometimes, I would just sit in silence like a good, old, and faithful dog.

## Chapter Seventeen

The patients on my assigned floor came and went. Some got better, some died, and two remained, week after week after week: Alice's mother, Nancy, the woman with the eleven IV bags (and the daughter who refused to give up) and Ed, the Jehovah's witness who was now in his last days. Each day my visits were about the same. Alice would be sitting next to her mother's bed, reading her the paper and having a one-way discussion about the latest current events. Nancy lay in the bed, almost unresponsive. Occasionally an eye would open and stare helplessly up at the ceiling. I would sit down in a chair next to Alice, and she would bring me up to date on her mother's condition. This report was always delivered with energetic enthusiasm about the latest little improvement that Alice had observed in the last twenty-four hours. Yesterday, her foot had moved.

The interns had taken over Nancy's care, and they were vigilant. I had heard that none of them wanted Nancy to die while she was in their care because they couldn't imagine the wrath of Alice. So, each day they were in her room calibrating, adjusting, and prescribing. I poked my head in.

"How's it going today, Alice?"

"Great! Mom talked today!"

"Really?" I took my usual seat. For ten minutes Alice went on and on about the latest treatments, drugs, and therapy her mother was getting and how it was all helping. I said my usual prayer: God, please help Nancy. I then made my escape and went over to my other chronic patient, Ed.

Ed's room was full of relatives. He was dying as a result of the refused transfusion.

The nurses had moved one of the beds out to make a large private room for him. They loved him. He looked like Santa Claus, and he had become like Santa Claus to the staff. He was always cheerful, loving, and warm. His room had become the break room. Staff would gather to wind down, to chat, and to get wise counsel from Ed. At first, his decision to forego the transfusion had caused the medical staff to spend most of their time trying to change his mind. Eventually, they realized that his mind was made up, and they respected him. He was being true to his religion.

Last week, Ed had told me how much he missed his wife. She had died less than a year ago, and not a day had gone by without Ed feeling her loss. He was happy at the prospect of joining her. Somehow, that piece of news made me feel okay with his decision, but I felt bad for Ed's son, Ed Junior. He was losing a second parent in just under a year, and he was angry. Every time I saw him, he was glaring at someone. The staff would scatter from his room like a flock of birds interrupted by a kid throwing stones. Ed Junior threw looks. He had a special one for me, full of disdain and disgust. Today he was standing outside his father's room, holding a bottle of water.

"Hey, Ed. How's your dad?"

"Awful. They're cleaning him up; he messed the bed."

"Oh, I'm sorry." I stood there with him, fingering my prayer rope. "He's a great guy, your dad."

Ed Junior began to cry. I put my hand on his shoulder, and he grabbed me in a bear hug. "I can't lose him too," he said into my hair. I held him, and then the nurse opened the door.

"You can go in now," she said.

Greeting cards and pictures covered the walls. Ed had a lot of friends, and they were all in pictures with him smiling and laughing. The man in the bed barely resembled the man in the pictures. He had lost a tremendous amount of weight, and his jolly round face had turned into a skeleton's mask. His breathing was labored.

The nurse lingered in the doorway. She looked at Ed Junior. "It probably won't be long now."

"Dad?" Ed Junior moved closer to the bed and put his hand on his father's. There was no response. I picked up his other hand.

"I don't think I can do this." Ed Junior looked over at me. "Will you stay with him? I don't want him to be alone."

"I can stay with him," I said. The monitor alarm went off. Ed's respirations were slowing. I reached up and shut it off.

"What's that?" Ed Junior looked up at the monitor.

"His breathing is slowing down."

"He's dying? Right now? I can't do this, I can't do this, I can't do this." Ed Junior was crying, but he had sat down on the chair beside his father's bed. We each held Ed's hands and waited. Tears fell down Ed Junior's face.

"Oh Dad, why do you have to go? I know you miss Mom, but what about me? I need you, Dad. I love you. I miss you." The respirations were getting slower with longer pauses between each breath.

"Tell him good-bye," I whispered.

"Good-bye, Dad, say hi to Mom," Ed said. Ed Senior took one more breath, exhaled slowly, and let go of life.

Ed Junior put his head on his father's chest and cried. I stroked the back of his head, repeating the Jesus prayer silently over and over. After a few moments, Ed got up and embraced me. "Thank you for being here with me. It was a holy moment. I think I felt some sort of peaceful presence. I can't believe he's gone, and I don't know what I'll do now, but I'm so glad I was with him when he died." We sat there together. Soon staff started to come to say good-bye to the man who had provided them with so much love and support over the past couple of weeks. It went on for a few hours, and it was comforting to Ed Junior. He began to see that his father wasn't crazy but a real force for love. And the love had left its mark.

## Chapter Eighteen

The only sound in the chaplain's office was the humming of the microwave reheating my coffee. I contemplated the remains of my dinner, wondering if I could get away with throwing out the fried fish in the office garbage can. The oil had already started to congeal on the leftover pieces encased in the now too-green tartar sauce. The office smelled like a diner. I set the microwave for another thirty seconds and gathered up the garbage.

As I started to back my way into the hallway, I noticed it was full of people emptying out of the hospital. It was past dinner, and they all seemed to be in a hurry to get out and enjoy the summer evening. I was daydreaming about a drippy ice-cream cone and a walk through the neighborhood when my pager went off. I pushed back open the office door and picked up the phone.

"This is the chaplain," I said as I watched the coffee boil over in the microwave.

"You're needed on the eighth floor." I heard crying in the background.

"I'll be right there." As I stood waiting for the elevators, I thought through all the possible scenarios that might await me on the critical care unit. If it was the eighth floor, it was bad. No one was in the process of healing there; they were all hanging on to life by a thread. The staff would be working desperately to strengthen the hold, but sometimes the thread just broke.

I could hear a child crying when I stepped off the elevator. Not the hysterical cry of someone who was hurt but a persistent cry that seemed to say something was very wrong. A woman was standing near the nurses' desk, holding a young boy over her shoulder. His arms were around her neck, and he was sobbing as if his heart was already broken. He kept repeating, "Are there, Mom? Are there?"

I walked past them to the nurse's station, and the unit secretary nodded at the woman and the boy. "They're the ones looking for the chaplain."

I approached the woman and touched her shoulder. "I'm the chaplain. Can I help?"

The mother put the boy down on the floor and knelt in front of him. "Here's the chaplain, Jess; she will know."

He stopped crying and looked up at me. I was getting the once over. I smiled and kneeled down in front of him.

"Do you have a question?" I asked.

He was still gasping a little from crying, and tears streamed down his face. "Yes." He focused his eyes on mine and took a deep breath. "Are there dinosaurs in heaven?"

At first, I thought I hadn't heard him correctly. I glanced at the mother. She was watching me and waiting.

"Are there dinosaurs in heaven?" I was buying time. He nodded. He was very serious, waiting like one awaits a verdict.

I had no idea what to say or even where to start. Who were these people? Why was he crying, and what was going on? Heaven questions usually meant someone was either dying or going to die soon. Please, God, help, I thought. What do I tell this little boy?

You were a sales rep, qualify him, said the voice in my head.

"Do you like dinosaurs?" I asked.

He thought for a moment then nodded slowly.

"Are they good dinosaurs or bad dinosaurs?"

He considered the question.

"Good dinosaurs," he said emphatically.

One last qualifying question, I thought. "If you were in heaven, would you want these dinosaurs with you?"

"Yes!"

"Well, then, yes, there are dinosaurs in heaven." I declared loudly.

He almost smiled, but he remained serious as he reached for his mother's hand. "See, Mom, Daddy will be okay."

But Daddy was far from okay. The young boy's father had been brought in about an hour ago. He had collapsed at a restaurant during dinner, and no one had been able to bring him around. He was still unconscious. The doctors were whispering the words brain aneurism. They were talking with the boy's mother about doing a brain scan.

"You mean he could be brain dead?" The mother was beginning to understand what the doctors were telling her. The young boy was sitting in the family waiting room with his older brother and sister. The children were watching anxiety build in the adults' faces.

"Yes, we would like to test him right now."

"Can the chaplain go in while you do the testing?" The mother grabbed my hand. "I just want you in there."

"Sure, I'll go," I said after I saw the doctor nod.

He was a big man. I had glanced at his chart while they were setting up the test. He was forty-six and looked healthy. His face was tan. He slept like someone taking a nap on a Saturday afternoon. His tan stopped at the shoulders, and I could almost picture him in a T-shirt with cut-off sleeves, throwing a baseball. His thick and curly reddish-blond hair spread out over the pillow. The ends were wet with sweat. It was as if he had been stopped in the middle of a pitch. His body laid down, and now for some unknowable reason, he was on life support.

The family went to the waiting room. Donna, the mother, needed a phone. She told me she had a large family. They would come and wait with her while I stayed with her husband, Greg.

I didn't watch the staff or the instruments. I held Greg's rough and calloused hand. Dirt had collected under the nails. The kind that was hard to scrub away. His hand was warm. It was the same hand that had probably grasped his wife's hand playfully as they had made their way into the restaurant, the kids running ahead. A fun summer evening out after a hard days work.

He was brain dead. Nothing could be done for him. The transplant team was called.

His hand had become heavy. I struggled to understand that the man "sleeping" in the bed was dead. The family had to be told.

The family waiting room overflowed with people, like people stuck at an airport. They sat wherever they could find a level spot on the floor and tables, and they ate snack food out of the vending machines. Kids ran around, and adults huddled in small groups, talking about what to do when there was nothing to do but wait.

Donna was at the center of the largest group of people. She sat on a small couch, an elbow on each knee and her head in her hands. Her long blonde hair made a curtain around her face.

"Donna?" I knelt in front of her.

She looked up at me, and her question was answered in my face. She put her arms around me and started to cry. The room got quiet.

"Mom?" It was the little boy. "Is Daddy in heaven?"

Donna leaned back and gathered up her son.

"Yes, Jess, Daddy is in heaven."

"With the dinosaurs?" he asked me.

"Yes, with the 'good' dinosaurs," I said. And then the dam broke. The group moved toward Donna, talking and crying all at once.

"When can we see him?" It was a voice from the group.

"We can go in a few at a time, but first the immediate family," I said.

Donna stood up and took Jess by the hand. Her fifteen-year-old daughter, Liz, and twelve-year-old son, Jake, had been huddling with one of Donna's sisters. She had seven brothers and sisters, and they were all there with their spouses and children.

In the room, Jess ran to his father's side.

"He's not dead. He's just sleeping!" He was excited. The grown-ups had made a terrible mistake. His father was obviously alive. His chest was visibly rising and falling like it always had when he was napping or trying to sleep in on a Saturday morning.

Donna stood with Liz and Jake, staring.

"It does look like he's sleeping, Jess, but your dad had something happen to his brain." I waited for Jess to take this in and the others too.

"His head's not hurt. There's no blood." Jess looked at me hopefully. He knew enough from TV and video games. There had to be blood.

"We can't see the blood. Your dad had bleeding on the inside of his head."

"But he's sleeping!" This was a cry of frustration and anger. Why couldn't everyone see that his father was sleeping peacefully in the bed? He couldn't be in two places at once. He was there stretched out in the bed.

I put my arms around Jess and guided him gently over to the bed. "Why don't you tell your daddy how much you love him? Then we'll go back in the other room and talk some more."

Donna and the other children came closer. "Let's pray," I said. I asked God for help.

The doctors came and explained to Donna and her family. Greg had bleeding in the brain. They were keeping him alive on life support. Did she want to donate his organs?

People were crying and holding one another in shock. Their lives had changed in a moment. The information was overwhelming. I called down to the kitchen and asked for a hospitality tray for forty people. They needed to eat and drink.

"Can you talk to these people?" It was the man from the organ transplant team. "We need a decision soon. There are people waiting for organs. He could save lives."

When the food came, I helped everyone find a seat and carried around the platter of cheese and crackers. Another person handed out water. It was quiet.

"Donna, are you willing to donate Greg's organs."

She looked at me with tear filled eyes. "I don't know. They would cut him up? I would get the pieces?" She shuddered.

"Just let him die peacefully. We'll go to him, pray, and let him go. We can all be with him." This was from a sister.

"But he could help other people; he could save lives." Another sister spoke up. They all looked like each other. They had the same wide eyes, same long hair, and the same athletic build.

The conversation raged, crashing into Donna like waves against a break wall. It went on for over an hour, pros and cons. She appeared to be listening, but she wasn't making any comments.

"What do you think we should do?" she asked me privately.

"Pray," I said.

"We're going to pray," she said.

They all stood like they had rehearsed this very moment, formed a circle, and held hands. I took Donna's hand on one side and Jake's hand on the other. Little Jess stood next to his mother, holding onto her leg.

"Please, God," I said, "help us." We all stood there, holding hands, waiting for God's help to come.

"God said to help other people," Jess said as he looked up at his mother. "Daddy helped other people all the time." He started to cry.

"Yes, Jess," she said, "You're right. We will help other people." She hugged him tight.

The family stood around Donna as she answered the myriad of questions from the transplant team. They needed to know if Greg smoked, how often he drank, what kind of exercise he did, what medications he was on, and what seemed like hundreds of other questions. When the interview was over and she was about to sign the consent form, Donna looked at the man from the transplant team and said, "I want his organs to stay local. I want to help someone from here."

"We can do that for everything but the heart and lungs. We don't do those kinds of transplants here, but we could make sure they go to the nearest place that does. Is that okay?" The man from the transplant team waited.

There was a pause, and then Donna said, "Yes." She signed away her husband's organs and put down the pen. "I need to say good-bye. Julie, can you take us?"

The four of us stood by the bed. Greg lay there oblivious to the drama happening around him. Donna kissed him on the lips. We half expected him to wake up like a fairy-tale prince, but he remained immobile other than the mechanical rhythmic rise and fall of his chest. Liz kissed his cheek, took her little brother by the hand, and pulled him toward the bed. Little Jess climbed up and laid on top of his father. "I love you, Daddy." Jess started to cry when Liz picked him up. They left with Donna. It was just Jake and I, Jake holding his father's hand while big tears rolled down the side of his face. The likeness between the man in the bed and the twelve-year-old boy was startling. The same red curls spread on the pillow lived on top of the boy's head.

"He's really dead? You saw?" Jake asked me. It was the first time he had spoken.

I nodded.

"But he doesn't look dead now, does he?"

"No, he doesn't look dead. They need to keep his body going so the organs won't die."

"Why does my dad have to die?" He looked at me as if I had this information but had decided not to share. "Why not some bad guy or some guy without kids? Why my dad?" He was angry. "There is nothing good about this."

I said nothing. Inside I was railing at God.

The family gathered and began moving out of the waiting area, leaving a pile of used cups, plates, and litter. A pizza box with only one piece missing was on one of the coffee tables, an unsuccessful attempt at dinner. It was now after midnight. One of her brothers was escorting Donna. He was carrying Jess while Liz and Jake followed. I watched Jake's face crumple in tears as the elevator doors shut.

At that moment, the transplant team wheeled out Greg's body. They were in a hurry. My pager went off.

I spent the rest of the night with the wife of a heart attack victim, who died after surgery. Her daughter arrived right after the death and took her mother out of my arms and out of the hospital. It was now morning and time for me to give my report as chaplain on call to my colleagues.

All I could think of was Jake's last remark. There is nothing good about this. It was like a mantra in my head as I replayed the night's events aloud for the group. I cried as I told them about Jess's dinosaurs, Donna's face, Liz's silence, and Jake's final remark. The group was silent and empathetic as they listened. Several of the women cried as I described how difficult it was for the children to understand that their father was dead and for them to say good-bye.

"So where is God in all of this?" Ted asked.

"Good question. God was certainly not there preventing the aneurism," I said. "I don't believe that God decides who is going to die of a brain aneurism. I know this stuff happens. I know that God doesn't interfere in our free will to make decisions, and it seems like God doesn't interfere in some of these biological events. So where does God come in? I just don't see where any good can come from this. I don't know what to think or do."

"I guess you'll just have to pray," Ted said.

"Okay, God, I need to know what good can come from this nightmare." My voice sounded sarcastic. I was at the end of my rope. We all got up to go. I made my way out of the room quickly before anyone could talk to me. I didn't want to talk; I was still raw from the experience. All I wanted to do was call my husband and get some sympathy before I started my day on the cancer floor. There was a bank of phones near the elevator. I started punching buttons. There was no answer on the house phone or either office phone. I slammed down the receiver when I heard a woman next to me crying. Three little kids surrounded her. Two were hanging on her skirts, and one was on her hip. She was crying as she spoke into the phone.

"I guess a man came in last night. His liver was a match, and they were able to do the transplant at about 2:00 a.m." She listened. "Dan would have died if it had been one more hour. They got him in just in time. I heard this man's organs saved seven people's lives." She glanced at me. I was staring at her, my eyes full of tears. Here was the good. The prayers had enabled the family to make the right decision. God had been working to make the best out of a horrible situation. My head was spinning from the events of the night. I couldn't get the images of the women with their children out of my head. One woman devastated with the loss of her husband. The other woman elated at the new life for her husband. But there was no time for contemplation; the shrill sound of my pager sounded as I plodded up the stairs. I needed coffee.

## Chapter Nineteen

The nurse was waiting for me at the doorway to the stairwell.

"This one is suicidal." She handed me a very thick chart. "I'm really worried about her, and I just don't have the time to sit and talk to her. She says she's bored, but I think she's really depressed. You have to help her." The nurse's name was Jane. I had talked with her a few times and knew she really cared about her patients. She pushed a few strands of hair behind her ear. Her face was wrinkled with worry.

"I'll try, Jane." She was already walking away.

The chart was for a female, twenty-two years old with an admitting diagnosis of acute Myeloid Leukemia. Her name was Jessica, and by the layers of paperwork, this was by no means her first trip to the hospital.

Jessica was sitting on her bed, eating a cheeseburger. The Burger King bag lay next to a hospital lunch tray that had not been touched. She squinted at my name tag and then lifted up the cheeseburger.

"It's from Jane," she said, motioning to the cheeseburger, "and you must be from Jane." She took another bite. Grease dripped onto her T-shirt and dribbled down onto her sweat pants. She dabbed at the spreading stain with a paper napkin.

"Oh, who cares?" She threw the napkin on the floor. She watched me pick it up. One of her eyes didn't seem to follow my movements. She brushed her fingers through her extremely short hair.

"I'm Julie, the chaplain." I threw the napkin in the trash and sat down.

"Oh really, and what do you do?"

I wondered if she was teasing me.

"I don't do anything; mostly I just listen to people, and lately I've been doing a lot of praying."

"Praying isn't going to help me." She put down the last bite of the cheeseburger.

"Oh yeah, why do you say that?" I got her a paper towel to wipe her hands.

"I have leukemia, and it's pretty bad. Besides that, I have asthma, allergies, and only one kidney." She sighed. "I've been in and out of hospitals since the day I was born."

"Wow, that's a lot to handle." Talk about an understatement, I thought to myself.

"Yeah, I thought I would try diabetes next." She laughed.

"So, which one are you in for this time?"

"I'm in for chemo again."

"Again?"

"For the leukemia. I've been in and out of the hospital since March." She paused and lowered her voice. "The nurses think I'm suicidal."

"Are you?"

"Well …" she got up from the bed. "Do you smoke?"

"Hold on, you've got to answer my question."

"I'm not suicidal, unless you think smoking is suicidal. It's not like I have lung cancer!" Her smile was more of a smirk. "Come downstairs with me, and I'll tell you more."

She was already fumbling with her pack of cigarettes when we were in the elevator. The volunteer at the front desk waved at her as we passed by.

I noticed a look of recognition on the valet's face. "You don't spend much time in your room, do you?"

"Nope, I spend a lot of time out here smoking. And I used to visit the other patients, but I've given that up." She was already lighting up.

"What made you stop visiting the other patients?" Her face suddenly looked older. She squinted, partly from the smoke and partly from the sun.

"Carl made me stop. Did you know Carl?"

"Yes, I knew Carl. I visited him too."

"I used to come into the hospital to see him. I met him back in March, and we became good friends. I spent a lot of time in his room, talking." She said this between drags. She inhaled deeply and slowly let the smoke spill out of her nose and mouth, almost inhaling it a second time. "Then he died." She stopped smoking and looked at me. "I felt horrible after he died. I got really depressed, and then they told me I had to come back here. So here I am."

"So, how are you now?" This was almost a rhetorical question. Jessica was slumped on the bench, staring at the ground, her cigarette's long ash about to fall.

"I'm pretty depressed." She looked away.

"Are you suicidal?" I touched her arm.

"No, I would never do it."

"Why not?"

She turned her entire body toward me and looked me straight in the eye. "I don't have the guts."

"I see." We sat in silence for a while. "So, what is it like to feel suicidal and not have the guts?" I asked.

"It feels like hell, and that's where I'm going when I die." She shrugged as if she was resigned to the idea.

"So, are you in hell right now?"

She stared off in the distance for a moment. "I guess so; it feels awful right now. God just won't give me a break. Everything in my life has been awful. I've been sick since the day I was born; my father beat me when I was a kid; I have a daughter, but my boyfriend started dating one of the staff he met when he was coming to see me back in March. We were going to get married, but now we're not. I just can't get a break. I'm in hell now, and I know I'm going there too." Tears formed in her eyes.

"How do you know that?" I asked as I searched my pockets for a tissue.

"Because I've done terrible things, and I know God doesn't love me because if he did, I wouldn't be in this mess. This is all punishment for all the horrible things I've done." She was nearly shouting. Several other smokers glanced in our direction.

"What kind of God is that? Certainly not the merciful God I know."

I spoke with intensity but lowered my voice.

"Well, what do you think God is doing?" She was standing now with her hands on her hips. "Reaching out to you." I stood.

"How? By giving me cancer?" She was incredulous.

"Do you think God gave you cancer?"

"No, I guess not. But you know, sometimes I see terrible things that could happen in the future." She was watching for my reaction.

"Really, can you give me an example?" We started walking back toward the hospital entrance.

"I was thinking about the future, and I saw a friend die in a car accident. I didn't want to say anything to him about it, so I didn't. Two weeks later, he died in a car accident. I could have prevented it. I think God told me this to help him, and I didn't help." She was openly sobbing as she told this story. "I want to know that God is really there."

I took her hand. "God is here, right now." Her hand was cold and lifeless. I put my arms around her and said in her ear, "God loves you."

"How do you know?" It was a whisper.

I let go of her and put my hands on both shoulders. "I know because of the countless stories of Jesus reaching out to people who didn't feel loved by anybody."

She just looked at me a moment and then said, "I'll have to think about that."

I watched her walk back into the hospital. The automatic doors closed behind her, and I saw her pack of cigarettes lying in front of the closed doors. She turned around, gave me a slight smile, and then disappeared down the hall.

## Chapter Twenty

Ted was late. I shifted from foot to foot, itching to get in his office and sit down. I had spent the past two hours at Nancy Walker's bedside, listening to her daughter, Alice, patter on about how her mother was going to beat the cancer. Nancy had been moved back to ICU. All her vital signs were slowing down. It was beyond a miracle that she was still alive.

I leaned against the wall, watching the parade of white lab coats march by, faces intent on something. No one acknowledged anyone else; they just kept moving. Their bodies taking them to their destination while their minds existed somewhere else. Sometimes I walked that way now too. I had no idea how I had gotten to Ted's office. My mind had stayed at Nancy's bedside, wishing I could somehow help her die.

Ted was next to me unlocking the office door.

"So, where were you just now?" he asked.

"Still at Nancy's bedside." I followed him in and sank down into the nearest chair.

"The mother who has cancer and the daughter who thinks she is going to beat it?"

"Yes!" I rolled my eyes. "I have never seen anyone with a better case of denial. I feel so bad for her mother. Every breath seems painful. She groans every time the nurses touch her."

"Uh huh." Ted sat in his chair. He was leaning forward like he was anticipating something.

"That's it? Uh huh? That woman is suffering!" I was now sitting on the edge of my chair.

"What woman?" Ted asked calmly.

What woman—was he deaf? I watched him take a tiny sip of his coffee. He sat back, eyes closed. The steam from his coffee made a lazy circle around the top of his mug.

What woman? His question hung in the air, and although I thought I knew the answer, I was unable to say it.

There was no question that the mother was suffering. She was a skeleton with tissue paper skin, veins clearly visible, raw bedsores at every pressure point despite the best efforts of the nurses. Every movement of her body caused her to groan. One day she was swollen with fluid; the next day she was dehydrated. She cried when she wasn't groaning. Her cries sounded like tiny baby birds whose mother had forgotten to feed them.

It was almost impossible to know what was going on with Alice. She was like a Stepford wife, programmed to think that her mother was immortal. And for some reason, she was able to discount all the evidence to the contrary. She was robotic in her responses, using the same phrases over and over. My mother will beat this. We need to help her. Mom, keep going. Don't give up. Day in and day out, for hours at her bedside, the same repetitive dialogue with anyone willing to listen. Her machinelike delivery gave no clue to any kind of feeling. Her eyes were empty.

Enough is enough, I thought, as I sat there watching Ted sip his coffee. "Okay, Ted, I'm the one suffering." As I said it, I knew it was true. Watching this woman die a slow and painful death reminded me of the time I saw a dog hit by a motorcycle. The dog was a young, beautiful husky. It bounded into the road while its owner screamed its name. The owner was running to catch the dog, a broken leash flopping around in his hand. The motorcycle swerved just as the dog veered in the same direction, and the dog was hit. It lay in the road, whimpering and howling, and all we could do was watch.

"I feel helpless. Isn't there anything they can do to alleviate her suffering?"

Ted put down his coffee cup. "You can alleviate her suffering."

"Me? How?" I didn't have any power. If the medical staff couldn't help her, how could I?

"Tell her daughter to let her mother go." Ted stood up and stretched.

"That's it? Just tell the daughter to let her mother go?" I stood up as well. I could see my time was up with Ted.

"Yes." Ted was already busy looking for something among the stack of file folders on his desk.

"So, I've had this power all along? It's my fault this poor woman is suffering because I didn't tell the daughter to let her go?" I touched his arm, and he turned to face me.

"Who knows, Julie? Who really knows when people are ready to hear things and when people are really ready to die? All you can do is try to help people along. It's not in your power; the choice is still their choice. But eventually, even Nancy's body will die in spite of her daughter. We do what we can." His blue eyes were full of compassion. "It's been a long haul with this one. Maybe if you're ready to tell the daughter, she might be ready to hear the message."

I nodded and left. I joined the parade of white coats marching in the direction of ICU.

Alice was in her normal spot. She was sitting in a straight-back chair next to her mother's bed, reading a magazine. The chair was between the bed and the wall. I stood behind her and peered down at the article. It was something about cancer survivors.

"Hey, Alice."

"Oh hi, Julie. I'm so glad you came back, I found the article I was telling you about this morning." She tried to hand me the magazine.

"I'm not here about the magazine. I came back to talk to you about your mother." Alice looked past me as if trying to figure out how she could escape.

"I don't want to talk about my mother with you." She moved toward me and made an attempt to step between the bed and me.

"Alice, just stop and listen." I blocked her with my body. "Your mother has cancer."

"No, no, no." Her hands were over her ears, and she had shut her eyes. Her face changed instantly from its empty shell to the look of a Halloween mask designed to show abject horror.

"In every organ of her body," I continued even louder.

"She is going to die, and it would be better if you let her go before she does."

Alice opened her eyes slowly and stared at me. Her empty eyes seemed to fill with color. They went from gray to blue to wet with tears. Her hands went from her ears to her eyes, and she started to sob. I took a step toward her, and she grabbed me like a drowning person. "Every organ?" she sobbed.

"Yes, every organ." I was struggling to stay standing. Her arms were around my neck, and her body had given way under the weight of the realization. She gradually got her feet back under her. After a few minutes, she clutched the rail of the hospital bed and pulled herself around to look at her mother. She seemed surprised to see all of the IV poles and bags. Her eyes caught sight of the monitor over the bed, and she watched the rhythm of her mother's heart for a few minutes. Her mother groaned.

"I don't want her to die." Alice suddenly looked panicked. "She can't die; I'm not ready to lose her." This was said right to her mother. She was leaning over the bed, trying to will her mother's survival.

"Alice, the woman is suffering." I was clear now who was suffering the most. At that moment, Nancy Walker let out a long, loud, throaty groan, and her face mirrored her daughter's expression of pain. Alice closed her eyes.

"Look, Alice, for heaven's sake, look at her face."

Alice opened her eyes and stared at her mother. "She is suffering."

"Tell her she can go, Alice." I took her hand. "It's okay; you can tell her she can let go."

"She can't hear me," Alice said, almost hopefully.

"She can hear you. Go ahead and tell her."

Alice closed her eyes again and asked softly, "Will you say a prayer first?"

"Sure." We moved closer to Nancy's head. I bent down close to her ear and pulled Alice with me. "Gracious and Holy God, set your servant Nancy free from all the bonds of this life so she can rest in your love. Amen."

Alice was crying as she bent down and kissed her mother's cheek. "You can go Mom; you can go."

I picked up her mother's hand and laid it in Alice's hand. We stood there for a few minutes. The crease lines in Nancy's face seemed to smooth out, and I could almost make out a slight smile. Her breathing seemed easier, and then her heart rate began to slow. An alarm went off. I heard the footsteps in the hall. "Alice? You need to let them know it's okay to let her go or they will resuscitate her." The mask of horror had returned to Alice's face and the peace that had settled in the room was shattered. The crash team was at the door.

"Alice?"

"Move, please," said a young intern who was leading the charge.

"Alice!" I looked over the back of the intern as he started to prepare to shock the heart of the dying woman. Nancy's heart rate was very slow, and her breathing was shallow.

Finally, I heard a high, squeaky "Stop."

I rapped the intern on his back. "Didn't you hear the daughter?"

"Huh," he grunted, still working feverishly to untangle the IV lines and heart monitoring leads.

"The daughter wants you to stop! She's letting her mother go." I was now pulling on his white lab coat.

The intern stood up and glared at me in disbelief. He turned to Alice. "Is this true?"

Alice was still holding her mother's hand, her head near her mother's head, and we could hear her saying over and over, "I love you Mom, I love you Mom, I love you Mom."

"I need her to tell me," the intern said. "Alice, do you want me to resuscitate your mother?"

"No! Let her die in peace."

The intern backed away from the bed. We stood there, almost suspended, hearing the beeping and the alarms of the monitors until one of the nurses turned them off. Suddenly, it was quiet. There were longer and longer pauses between Nancy's breaths. She let out one last sigh before there was stillness. Alice didn't move. None of us moved until the intern began to cry. Alice went over and held him.

I stared at the sight of this unlikely pair sharing a moment of grief. The intern's young face was buried in Alice's shoulder.

"I'm sorry," he murmured. "I'm so sorry."

One of the nurses whispered to me. "Doesn't he know she had cancer all through her body?"

I shrugged. "Dr. Carlson?" I tapped him on his shoulder. "You need to call time of death."

He turned toward me. He looked as if I had just woken him up after only an hour of sleep. "Me?" he asked.

"Yes, have you ever done this before?"

"Uh, no, but I think I know what I'm supposed to do."

I glanced over at Alice. She had taken her usual spot next to her mother's bed. Her eyes were closed, and her head was down.

The young Dr. Carlson took his stethoscope out of his pocket and listened to Nancy's chest. He was methodical in his search for a heartbeat. The room had gradually cleared of people, and it was now just the three of us waiting for those final official words. Alice opened her eyes.

"Time of death," Dr. Carlson squinted at the clock on the wall, "4:00 p.m." It was finally over for Nancy.

It was only beginning for Alice. The two of us sat with the body, me on one side and Alice on the other side, each holding one of Nancy's hands. We prayed and talked as Nancy grew colder and the softness of life gradually gave way to the stiffness of death. Alice's family came and went, saying their good-byes to Nancy and then whispering to me how hard this was going to be on Alice. They said Alice was so close to her mother and that this had been her life the past few months.

At 9:00 p.m. the last family member left. Alice had told them all to go on without her. She wasn't ready to leave, and she didn't want to feel pressured. The staff had called the funeral home, and they were due any minute. The social worker had informed me that they needed the hospital room and that five hours was more than enough time to say good-bye to a loved one.

Nancy lay motionless underneath the sheet. She was totally covered with just her head exposed. I could see the outline of her crossed arms under the sheet. Alice stared at her mother's face as if willing her back to life.

"Alice, we need to go now." I crossed over to her side of the bed and put my hand gently on her back.

"I don't know how to leave her."

"You aren't leaving her; she had to leave you." I took Alice's hand and pulled upward.

"I don't think I can go." Her hand was lifeless. I had to grip it hard. I pulled a little harder.

"Stand up, Alice." She stood. Thank God, I thought. We gradually inched ourselves away from the body. I had already said every prayer for the dead and every prayer for the grieving family that I could. I could think of nothing left to do for Alice other than to help her out of that room and down to the parking garage.

I guided her out of the room, down the hall, and into the elevator. It was like leading a partially paralyzed blind person. I was afraid she was just going to collapse and melt onto the floor. After the silent ride down, we walked through the lobby and out to where her husband was waiting in the car. I reached to open the passenger door, and Alice grabbed me. She had started to fall, and then it came.

The tears were like a sudden thunderstorm. In one second, she was screaming, crying, and moaning. She clutched me like a drowning person, squeezing the air from my lungs. Her cries were so intense that she was literally gasping for air.

"Breathe, Alice, just breathe. Just get to the next breath. One breath at a time." I had never lived so profoundly in the moment. We were just surviving from one breath to the next, and nothing else mattered. I could almost see us from above. One woman slumped in another woman's arms, both just focused on taking the next breath and making it to the next moment. It took quite a lot of breaths, and then she was done. Alice pulled herself up, grasped the door handle, opened it, and climbed in.

"God bless you." I whispered as I closed the door for her. I watched as the car disappeared around the corner of the garage. I stared at my feet. The pavement was wet with her tears.

Somehow, I made my way to the chapel. I sat in the front row and stared up at the mosaic. It was the twenty-third Psalm. "Yea though I walk through the valley of the shadow of death, I will fear no evil, for thou art with me." It had been a long walk. What had kept us going was the breath of life that comes unbidden to us that we are barely conscious of until we watch it leave someone else.

# Acknowledgments

It has now been fifteen years since I completed a unit of Clinical Pastoral Education in preparation for my ordination in the Episcopal Church. I continue to give thanks for this experience that formed me as a person of prayer.

I am most grateful to my family who supported me during the three months of the program, especially my husband, Scott, who was always there to offer words of encouragement and our children, Kenny, Eric, Tommy, Chaz and Kyle who were a great source of blessing at the time and today!

Thank you to my team at Hewlett-Packard for covering for me and praying for me during my three-month chaplaincy. A special thanks to Mary Ann Griffith for hiring me and giving me this gift of time.

I would not have completed this project if it weren't for a chance meeting of Douglas Hixson, who took the book on as an editing project. His additions brought many of the scenes alive that were sorely lacking in description.

My Aunt Janice Moore agreed to keep me on schedule as I struggled to complete my last edits.

Richard Neslund provided me with incredible feedback, provocative questions, spectacular images, and words of encouragement. It was your gracious responses that pushed me over the tipping point to push through to the end.

I am grateful to all the people who I visited during my chaplaincy for their patience and their willingness to let me witness these profound moments of their lives. However, the stories are my experience.

I am most grateful for the Rev. Dr. Tyler Dudley who was my CPE supervisor and shepherded me through the program. He taught me how to pray.

## *About the Author*

Julie Cicora is an Episcopal priest working on the bishop's staff in the Diocese of Rochester as the canon for mission and ministry. She received her master of divinity at Colgate Rochester Divinity School and was ordained in 2000 after a twenty-two-year career at Hewlett-Packard in sales. She lives in upstate New York with her husband and spends time visiting her five sons and four granddaughters.

Made in the USA
Middletown, DE
18 June 2015